German General Staff
Barry Leach

BB

Editor-in-Chief: Barrie Pitt
Editor: David Mason
Art Director: Sarah Kingham
Picture Editor: Robert Hunt
Consultant Art Editor: Denis Piper
Maps and charts: Graham Bingham

Photographs for this book were especially selected from the following
archives: Bundesarchiv, Koblenz; Rikjksinstituut, Amsterdam; United States
National Archives; West Coast Picture Archive; Blackstar Publishing, London;
Radio Times, Hulton Picture Library, London; Ullstein, Berlin;
Staatsbibliothek, Berlin; Imperial War Museum, London; Barry Leach and
General Siewert.

First Printing: August 1973

Printed in United States of America

Ballantine Books Inc.
201 East 50th Street, New York, N.Y. 10022

Contents

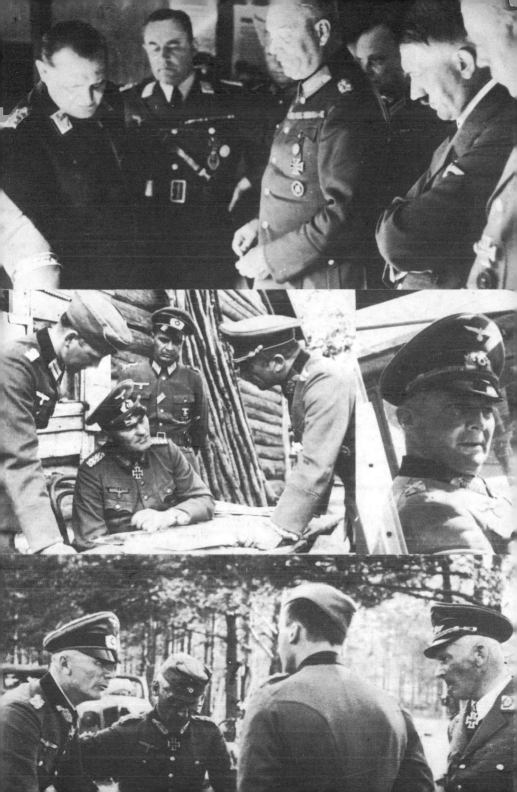

Select Company

Introduction by Barrie Pitt

It is difficult if not impossible to think of any organisation either inside or outside the military world, which attained more prestige than the German General Staff. The *Grand Quartier Général* was regarded by 1914 as a sycophantic joke even in an army with a higher opinion of itself than any other in the world, while the British Imperial General Staff, whatever its performance, could never vie in popular esteem or world-wide regard with the Admiralty. And even the controlling organisation of the Royal Navy was outshone by that of the *Heer*, the *Reichswehr* or the *Wehrmacht* – or whatever other name the German Army accepted – possibly because the individual members of the latter worked inconceivably harder than those of the former.

Prussian industry has always been a quality which the rest of the world has regarded with awe, hiding the fear which it engenders behind a curtain of irreverence – and the stories of prolonged mental and physical effort by members of what eventually became known as OKH are legion and well-authenticated. Perhaps the archetypal chief was von Schlieffen who welcomed holidays as times when he and his staff could concentrate on problems without the interruptions of

daily routine, and one Christmas Eve gave each of them a task to solve over the festive season. One of them (possibly Ludendorff) wishing to see something of his family at that time of the year, worked all night and handed in his solution on Christmas morning – to be rewarded for his industry with another problem of even greater complexity to keep him engaged during the time which must elapse before resuming normal duties.

And the daily routine of General Halder, perhaps the most successful and certainly the most tenacious of Hitler's Chiefs of Staff, upholds the tradition. As readers of this absorbing study will learn '. . . he rose at five and went horse riding until seven thirty. After breakfast he received the morning reports from the field army, then heard the views of his section heads and discussed the current situation. He then received liaison officers until about eleven o'clock. For the next hour he conferred with various subordinates on a great multiplicity of administrative matters until noon when they went to lunch. He did not eat lunch but used the next hour to read through the mass of papers which accumulated on his desk. Then the flow of visitors began again until dinner between 8 and 9 pm after which the Chief of Staff refreshed himself for the next round of work by taking a short sleep. He then worked on his correspondence and his notebook into the night until 2.30 am or later.'

As he had also frequently to attend conferences and listen to diatribes from an increasingly fractious Führer, his normal facial expression of intense irritability can be explained – but there have been many armies in which a man capable of such prolonged effort would not be welcome, and would not rise to high rank if he gained admittance.

Perhaps herein lies the secret of the respect with which the German General Staff has always been regarded; it was a serious controlling organisation in charge of a serious army which was itself regarded as epitomising the aspirations and hopes of a serious nation. It was therefore a most potent factor in world politics, and sometimes gave the impression of being a force in itself.

This impression was of course misleading, as without the army it controlled the General Staff was nothing, and its training and philosophy insisted that it was an instrument of policy and not in itself a policy-maker. This attitude is undoubtedly the most practical in a world which has learned the hazards and discomforts of military dictatorships, but what happens to an organisation composed mostly of honourable professionals when the members discover that fate has made their organisation the tool of a criminal maniac?

This was the situation which confronted the German General Staff once the armies they controlled had swept deep enough into Russia to give Hitler confirmation of his visions of personal world supremacy, and his creatures opportunity to put into practice the abominable theories which made up so large a part of Nazi philosophy

Di Leach's admirable account of the strains to which the General Staff was subject, of the ways in which they attempted to restrain the worst excesses of their political master and the way in which he in turn restricted their influence and powers, polluted their company and ideals with sycophants and deceit and forced them to decimate their own ranks after the bomb attempt on his life, makes one of the most important books in this series, and will undoubtedly become a classic work of reference on this complicated but enthralling subject.

The Proud Tradition

On 15th October 1935 the leading generals of the Third Reich gathered in Berlin for the reopening of the *Kriegsakademie* The ceremony took place in the renovated barracks formerly occupied by the First Guards Field Artillery Regiment on the Lehrterstrasse near the site of the old staff academy which had been founded by Scharnhorst exactly 125 years earlier. In 1920 the *Kriegsakademie* had been closed and the Great German General Staff dissolved by the Treaty of Versailles. Thus the opening ceremonies presented an opportunity to celebrate the end of an era of humiliation and the revival of a German army and General Staff free from irksome restrictions.

The guests for the occasion represented both the hopes for the future of the Reich and the proud traditions of the past. The Führer himself was present as Supreme Commander of the Armed Forces. He was attended by Propaganda Minister Josef Goebbels, Interior Minister Wilhelm Frick and the usual retinue of Nazi officials. Hermann Göring and Erhard Milch were also there, showing off the brand new uniform of the Luftwaffe. In striking contrast was the aged figure of Field-Marshal von Mackensen in the full dress uniform of the Death's Head Hussars. Another representative from the past was General Hans von Seeckt. The features behind his immaculately clipped white moustache and gleaming monocle were impassive. But he must have felt some emotion on this day, especially when the Commander-in-Chief of the Army, General Werner Freiherr von Fritsch saluted him with the words: 'The General Staff which has revived since the collapse carries into its very youngest generation the stamp of your personality, Herr Generaloberst'. For it was Seeckt who had maintained the traditions and methods of the General Staff in the command structure of the Reichswehr which he had painstakingly built upon the ruins of the old Imperial Army in the 1920s.

The active military leaders sitting around him had been majors and colonels then. Blomberg, Fritsch, Beck, Rundstedt, Witzleben and Liebmann were all generals now. Generals he had trained and prepared for this revival. But if the army owed him a debt of gratitude, it owed even more to the former lance-corporal and regimental runner who occupied the place of honour on this auspicious occasion.

It was to Adolf Hitler that General Liebmann, Commandant of the Academy, addressed his opening remarks: 'This memorial day comes in the year in which one of the restricting bonds of the Versailles Treaty has been torn away by your actions on 16th March (the reinstitution of compulsory military service), and the German people have been given again their freedom of arms . . . We realize . . . that we have solely your determination and will and your infallible leadership to thank for our freedom and – like the German people – we and the entire German Wehrmacht will show our thanks to you, our Führer, through unflinching faithfulness and devotion'.

The major address was given by the War Minister, General von Blomberg, who praised Scharnhorst as the founder of the German General Staff and of the *Kriegsakademie*, and as a revolutionary who had established 'the unity of the People, the State and the Armed Forces'. The parallels between the revival of Prussia after its humiliating defeat at the hands of Napoleon in 1806 and the revival of Germany after the defeat of 1918 were enthusiastically stressed throughout the War Minister's speech.

The next speaker also drew from history for his theme. But as befitted the Chief of the General Staff of the Army, Ludwig Beck spoke in an aca-

Blomberg, Mackensen and Hitler on the occasion of a visit to the Great War Memorial in Berlin

Leading generals gather in Berlin for the reopening of the *Kriegsakademie*, October 1935

demic tone, taking as his theme a dictum of his most eminent predecessor, von Moltke the Elder, 'genius is work'. Somewhat contradicting Blomberg, Beck stated that the defeat of 1918 was not, as in 1806, a military failure. The German army had returned from the front 'crowned with laurels of immortality'. Thus the Reichswehr's task had not been to find new methods but to preserve those elements which contributed to 'the tremendous military superiority of the old army'. In the opinions of Beck and his fellow generals the most important of those elements was the German General Staff.

As the speakers on 15th October 1935 indicated, the great traditions of the German General Staff had their roots in the era of reform which followed the defeats inflicted upon the Prussians by Napoleon in 1806 on the fields of Jena and Auerstadt. Prior to that time there had been attempts to develop a general staff, but it had been bereft of influence by the noble military adjutants around the royal Commander-in-Chief, the King of Prussia. It was, 'compared to that of France, a mere shadow of a general staff'. The task of giving it substance fell mainly to Gerhard Johann Scharnhorst, to whom the Prussian defeat revealed the need for social as well as military reform. Only by abolishing serfdom and encouraging national enthusiasm and a sense of duty could an army be drawn from the State to defend it against aggression. Thus the Military Reorganisation Commission set out, in the words of Scharnhorst, 'to bring the army and the nation into a more intimate union'. This could be achieved by introducing conscription and identifying the citizen's period of service under arms as the final stage in his education. Thus the Prussian army was regarded, with the family and the school, as a pillar of the State.

In order to justify this new role, education rather than noble birth now became the chief qualification for a commission. Like conscription, the opening of the officer corps to the middle-class was strongly criticised by the royal and noble officers who sought to persuade the King that qualities other than learning were essential to the exercise of command. Nevertheless, in 1810 a number of military schools offered courses to prepare candidates for a commission. At the same time the *Kriegsakademie* was opened in Berlin to provide selected officers with the knowledge of tactics, strategy, military technology, map-reading, geography, languages and administration required for higher command. The best pupils were appointed to the General Staff.

The need for a trained body of general staff officers was the result of the increase in the size of armies and their organisation into separate divisions and corps. For both logistical and strategic reasons these formations usually marched separately and united only to do battle. Much of Napoleon's success was due to his swift marches to achieve a concentration of force which could overwhelm the still dispersed formations of his opponents. To do this an army commander needed a staff capable of collecting and assessing intelligence about the enemy's location and possible intentions. Such intelligence then had to be coordinated with the movements of his own formations. This, in turn, required staffs at each formation headquarters trained in uniform methods of responding efficiently to the orders of the army commander. Thus Scharnhorst formed the *Grosser Generalstab* at royal headquarters, while the staffs of the formation headquarters comprised the *Truppengeneralstab*.

In addition to providing a system of command, the general staffs at formation headquarters were a means by which encouragement or restraint could be exercised on the field commanders, many of whom were stubborn nobles or *Landwehr* colonels with more patriotic enthusiasm than military experience. At the highest level Chiefs of Staff like Gneisenau, Boyen, Grolman and Clausewitz became even more renowned than their Commanders, Blücher, Bülow, Kleist and Thielmann.

When Scharnhorst died of a septic wound in 1813 he was succeeded by August Wilhelm von Gneisenau. The new Chief of the General Staff instituted the important practices of 'joint responsibility' and 'general directive'. The first meant that a chief of staff shared responsibility with his commander for the decisions expressed in orders. In cases of disagreement a chief of staff could communicate his views directly to the Chief of the General Staff. This measure strengthened the spirit of unity in the general staff corps and enabled its members to assert their collective authority over irresponsible or inefficient commanders. At the same time, Gneisenau avoided rigidity by extending Frederick the Great's system of directives. Subordinate commanders were issued with directives expressing the intent

The Founder – Scharnhorst

13

The Exponent – Gneisenau

The Philosopher of War – Clausewitz

of the Royal Headquarters in terms of clear objectives but giving only general indications of the methods for their achievement. This enabled commanders and their staffs to use initiative in taking advantage of unforeseen opportunities, provided that their actions were consistent with the main objective.

For Gneisenau the main objective was usually the destruction of the enemy army. The Prussian preference for *Vernichtungsstrategie* has often been cited as a proof of brutality. In fact it was based upon the military-geographical realities of the location of Prussia's territories, scattered and exposed across the centre of Europe. Unable to wage wars of attrition like Great Britain, conduct strategic withdrawals like Russia, or engage in diplomatic juggling for a balance of power like Austria, Prussia had little choice but to inflict a decisive defeat upon an adversary or suffer occupation and dismemberment. Further-more, the Prussians rapidly learned from their bitter experiences fighting Napoleon that if a beaten army is allowed to escape from the battlefield it can quickly revive and strike back.

As a result when Karl von Clausewitz, the pupil and colleague of Scharnhorst and Gneisenau, came to formulate the lessons of war in his monumental work, *Vom Krieg*, he recognised that the French Revolution and Napoleon had brought in a new age which demanded a more ruthless form of war. Dynastic politics, balance of power diplomacy and chess-board strategy were over. The survival of nation-states was now the issue. Like his contemporary, Hegel, the Prussian court philosopher, Clausewitz regarded the State as the embodiment of man's supreme achievement on earth. He believed that only through the State could the individual achieve his truest freedom and only in the service of the State could the individual citizen claim worth. And since his supreme duty was the defence of the State, the army embodied all that was best and truest in the State. Since the State could not exist undefended Clausewitz believed that the survival of the army had priority over that of the State. These views formed the basis of the philosophy which guided the Prussian and German General Staff Corps in the 19th and 20th centuries. It is essential to remember this if we are to under-stand the behaviour of the German Army leaders at those times during the Weimar Republic and the Third Reich when the interests of the army seemed more important to them than those of the State or its citizens.

A similar lack of humanity also

seemed to be implied in Clausewitz's cold statement that the more war '. . . embraces the whole existence of peoples, . . . the more its purpose will be to hurl the enemy to the ground, the more purely warlike, the less political will war appear to become.' Nevertheless, Clausewitz recognised war not only as 'an act of violence pushed to its utmost bounds', but also as a 'continuation of political trans-actions intermingled with different means'. Thus war could be justified only if it achieved the aims of policy. The soldier must serve the statesman, not usurp him. He must share with the statesman the task of selecting the point against which to concentrate military operations. This would nor-mally be the enemy army. But Clause-witz also recognised that if the enemy state suffered from internal weaknes-ses the capital city or 'public opinion' may become 'a vital military objec-tive'. This suggested that 'limited' war might provide an alternative to 'absolute' or 'total' war. But the waging of limited war would require a rare combination of political, dip-lomatic and military skills. When

Bismarck and Moltke achieved such a combination, the Prussian General Staff won its greatest distinction.

Moltke became Chief of the General Staff in 1857. At that time the post had lost some of its prestige. The direct access to the King enjoyed by Scharn-horst and Gneisenau had been taken away, and the General Staff was sub-ordinated to a branch of the War Ministry. Nevertheless, staff duties had been systematised, and were rigorously practised on staff field tours (*Generalstabsreisen*) and annual army manoeuvres. Historical, Map-ping and Survey, and Railway Sections had been added to the General Staff. As might be expected in the 19th century, war became 'scientific' and more dependent upon industry. It was the railway network which gave Moltke the means he needed to swiftly mobilize and concentrate the large army made available by conscription.

Moltke first impressed his superiors in the war against Denmark in 1864, but it was two years later, in the Austro-Prussian war, that he gave the

Moltke dictates the surrender terms

that they converged upon the front and flank of the Austrian army at Sadowa.

On the eve of this great battle when one of the divisional commanders had received his orders, he remarked 'This is all very well, but who is General Moltke?' After Sadowa this question was never asked again. Moltke's name was renowned, for he had achieved Clausewitz's ideal – the decisive victory by means of a battle of destruction. Four years later he repeated this performance by annihilating the army of the Emperor Napoleon III at Sedan. But this battle did not end the Franco-Prussian War; the struggle dragged on for several months. After the war Moltke tried to discourage the General Staff from using decisive battles as the basis for a 'system' of strategy. He also warned that however precise the planning there are always elements of chance in war which make nonsense of preconceived 'scientific' solutions to strategic problems. Furthermore, the success of the wars against Austria and France resulted not only from the military victories but also from the consumate skill with which Bismarck used diplomacy to isolate the victims and to negotiate peace when the soldiers' work was done.

In spite of these considerations, Moltke in his last years in office began to use the enormous prestige and power of the General Staff to advocate a preventive war against Russia or France. Bismarck, now retired, fretted to see his policy of alliances endangered, and wrote in his memoirs that 'the General Staff's desire for a preventive war had its origin in the spirit which such an institution was bound to foster, and which he for his part did not wish to see it lack. The only question was what would happen when you got an aggressive Chief of the General Staff in combination with a weak and incompetent Monarch and a Chancellor without political per-

most devastating demonstration of the precision of his mobilization plans and the efficiency of his staff system by deploying the Prussian armies so

Kaiser Wilhelm II with Moltke

a particular valley, he remarked laconically, 'An unimportant obstacle'. It was for this cold, detached, narrow professionalism that Schlieffen was regarded as the doyen of the General Staff. In the eyes of his colleagues his 'imposing personality' seemed to embody the highest standards of duty and efficiency developed by the General Staff in the 19th century. But in fact the qualities possessed by Schlieffen were adequate only for the performance of purely military staff duties at the army command level involving questions of tactics, and military strategy. As Chief of the General Staff and senior military adviser to the Kaiser, Schlieffen and his successors entered the realm of grand strategy. Scharnhorst and Moltke had been equal to the task of relating military operations to the needs of policy, but Schlieffen was not. In fairness to Schlieffen it must be said that the liberation of Prussia and the unification of Germany presented Scharnhorst and Moltke with clear tasks and strong political and popular support, but in the Wilhelmian Reich the General Staff had become isolated from the people and from the politicians. It was confronted with a complex international situation in which it was more difficult than in 1813 or 1870 to define or justify offensive aims. In the absence of clear political direction, it was perhaps inevitable that the Chief of the General Staff should take advantage of his power and prestige to propose a military strategic solution to the grand strategic problem posed by the real and imagined 'encirclement' of Germany.

It fell to his successor, the younger Helmuth von Moltke, to put Schlieffen's Master Plan into practice. The doubts he had expressed before the war about the practicability of exercising control over the vast operation were justified by events. The offensive collapsed through a lack of

spective and without authority'. Bismarck's question was answered in 1914 when the German General Staff set the Schlieffen Plan in motion and invaded Belgium.

A century earlier Clausewitz had warned: 'It is an inadmissible and even harmful distinction to leave a great military enterprise or its planning to a 'purely military judgement'. Yet this is exactly what occurred in the Wilhelmian Reich when Count Alfred von Schlieffen developed his Master Plan. The words 'purely military' exactly describe Schlieffen. His mind and energies were utterly devoted to his profession. He sent his subordinates military problems on Christmas Eve and expected the answer on Boxing Day. When, on a staff field tour, his attention was drawn to the beauty of

The Russian Peace Delegation arrives at
German HQ at Brest-Litovsk

**The Russian Peace Delegation arrives at
German HQ at Brest-Litovsk**

confidence and control at General
Headquarters. Moltke's successor,
Erich von Falkenhayn attempted to
limit operations to a more manage-
able size. In doing so he prevented
Hindenburg from taking full advantage of his victories on the Eastern
Front. Like Schlieffen he staked all
upon a decisive battle in the West.
But Verdun was a battle of attrition
not manoeuvre, and the Germans paid
in human lives as dearly as the
French. Finally, Hindenburg became
Chief of the General Staff, with Erich
Ludendorff as Quartermaster-General
adding ruthless brilliance and dynam-
ism to the old Field-Marshal's stability and common sense.

Hindenburg and Ludendorff had
won their reputations by their military strategy and direction of operations in the East. But they were
unable to solve the grand strategic

problems. Their ruthless mobilization of Germany's material resources achieved remarkable increases in war production but imposed unbearable strains upon the civil population. The proclamation of an independent Poland provided a new ally for the Central Powers, but it destroyed hope of a negotiated peace with Tsarist Russia. The use of unrestricted U-boat warfare was intended to knock Britain out, but it brought the United States into the war. The General Staff's meddling in internal politics served only to weaken further the political leadership of the State. The deliberate fostering of revolution in Russia unleashed a wave of Bolshevik propaganda upon their own troops retained in the East to enforce the draconian peace imposed on Russia at Brest-Litovsk. Finally, Ludendorff re-

General Falkenhayn, centre, commanding Ninth Army on the Rumanian front, on his way to the trenches

sorted to the same military strategic solution attempted by the Schlieffen Plan, a great offensive in the West. The decision was made in an army group headquarters at a meeting between Ludendorff and the chiefs of staff of the army groups in the West. Ludendorff was not in the least concerned that the Kaiser, the Imperial Chancellor and Ministers were excluded from the decision-making process. Colonel Bauer wrote later that the First Quartermaster-General's strategic plans 'had, of course, to take the political and economic situation into account. But his views and his economic and political plans found no support in the government . . . to Ludendorff all political questions were military questions'. Thus Ludendorff believed that a 'military victory' would 'shake the position of Lloyd George and Clemenceau' and 'make the enemy inclined to peace'. While the grand strategic aims of Ludendorff's offensive were vague, and the military strategic intentions un-

German Guard-Dragoon regiment advances during the great offensive in the West

From left to right: Field-Marshal
Mackensen, General Ludendorff, a staff
officer, Hindenburg and Seeckt, Head of
the Reichswehr and architect of the
Wehrmacht

defined, the tactical, technical and
administrative preparations were
masterly. The detailed planning and
preparations were rewarded with
great successes, but the effects of
these were dissipated through the
lack of a clear strategic priority. The
failure of Ludendorff's offensive in 1918
forced him to admit that the war
must be ended. He told the Kaiser
that he had 'no hope of finding a strategic expedient whereby to turn the
situation to [Germany's] advantage'.

In fact, for four years of the most
gruelling warfare in history the
officers of the German General Staff
had sustained the Central Powers by
a whole series of expedients. But their
sheer military virtuosity could not
compensate for the lack of political
direction and grand strategic objectives, and enable them to win the war.
Nevertheless, it enabled them to
defeat Russia, and to make it very
difficult for the Allies to win. Furthermore, the revolution which spread
through Germany in the Autumn of
1918 enabled the Army to assert that
the German collapse was the result of

a 'stab in the back'. Thus the proud
traditions of the German General
Staff managed to survive even the
humiliation of defeat.

Looking back over the years between the wars, Colonel Hermann
Foertsch of the General Staff com-
mented that '. . . lost wars call more
insistently for examination than
those that have been won. They never
let you rest, and they force you to
reflect, while victories harbour the
danger that lies in the self-confidence
of the victor.' The study of the lessons
of the First World War was a challenging task for any army, but for
Germany it was made doubly difficult
by the clause of the Treaty of Versailles which forbade the reinstitution
of the Great General Staff and all
similar organisations, including the
Kriegsakademie. The man who over-
came this problem and thus lay the
foundation for the future expansion of
the German Army was General von
Seeckt.

Hans von Seeckt was a general staff
officer of outstanding reputation. As
Chief of Staff to Mackensen he had
directed operations at Gorlice in 1915
and in Rumania in 1916 with masterly
skill. In the latter part of the war he
had helped to bolster the resistance
of Germany's south-eastern allies by
serving on the Austrian and Turkish

General Staffs. When the Reichswehr of 100,000 men was established von Seeckt was appointed Chief of the General Troop Office (*Allgemeine Truppenamt*), a section of the Reichswehr Ministry which performed some of the central functions of the General Staff. On 6th July 1919 he sent a directive to all General Staff officers containing the words: 'The form changes, the spirit remains as before. It is the spirit of silent, selfless performance of duty in the service of the Army. General Staff officers have no name.' In a further directive on 18th October 1919 Seeckt showed that the General Staff Corps of the Reichswehr would uphold old traditions and set new standards of efficiency: 'I expect every General Staff officer to ensure that by unremitting effort he acquires the highest possible degree of military ability and exerts upon the entire army an exemplary, inspiring and stimulating influence. Steadfast in concern for the troops . . . it will be his aim to make of them not only a reliable pillar of the State but also a

In March 1920, a coup d'état, manoeuvred by Dr Kapp, momentarily succeeds

school for the teachers and leaders of the Nation. . . . As such you (general staff officers) must stand above parties and factions, then we shall have our hands and our hearts free for work embracing the whole people.' Seeckt's

General Gröner, Ludendorff's successor, helps to preserve the old army in the new Republic

Seeckt with men he trained for command: Generals Busch, *left,* and Fritsch, *right*

view was not shared by all the officers of the Reichswehr. Early in 1920 some of them supported the Kapp *Putsch,* an abortive attempt to overthrow the Republic, led by right-wing politicians and bureaucrats and the impetuous General Lüttwitz. As a result of

achievement of this aim was the preservation of the spirit and traditions of the old General Staff. Seeckt therefore retained among the 4000 officers permitted to the Reichswehr a very high proportion of members of the old General Staff. Several sections of the General Staff itself were dispersed among the civil ministries. The Topographical Section went to the Ministry of the Interior, the Rail-

Seeckt with men he trained for command: Generals Busch, *left,* and Fritsch, *right*

the crisis von Seeckt was appointed *Chef des Heeresleitung* (Chief of Army Direction).

Once he was virtually Commander-in Chief, von Seeckt sought to make the Reichswehr an army of leaders, an élite force which at every level could provide a framework for expansion. The most important step towards the

Dummy tanks in use during *Reichswehr* manoeuvres

General Otto Hasse issues orders during manoeuvres

way Section to the Ministry of Transport (where its officers found their former Chief, General Gröner, as Minister), and the Military History Section disappeared into the new government archives. The Foreign Office took over aspects of Intelligence work, and the Ministry of Pensions handled some of the work of the

Personnel Office. Retired and active members of the General Staff corps' were able to meet and discuss problems of mutual interest at their own club, the *Verein Graf Schlieffen*. Special courses for senior staff officers were given in Berlin to bring them up to date with the latest developments in military thought, politics and economics.

While these measures enabled trained staff officers to continue their work, they made no provision for the training of new ones. The *Kriegsakademie* was specifically banned by the Treaty of Versailles, so Seeckt made each of the seven military districts responsible for conducting general staff training on the basis of directives issued by the Training Section (T4) of the *Truppenamt*. The Military District Examination was taken simultaneously by all officers of the Reichswehr between twenty-five and thirty years old. The best ten candidates in each Military District were given two years staff training, euphemistically called 'assistant leaders training' (*Führergehilfenausbildung*). After a final exam the best ten or fifteen officers from the whole army were sent for a third year of training in the Reichswehr Ministry in Berlin.

Applied Tactics was regarded as the most important paper of the Military District examination, which also included papers on Tactical Theory Weapons, Fieldcraft, Engineering and eight general subjects including a foreign language. Three or four problems had to be answered in a period of six to ten hours. They were usually based on the operations of an infantry regiment reinforced with elements of other arms, and involved the presentation of the regimental commander's appreciation of the situation and the orders, organisation and other measures resulting from his decisions. Together with his examination results, the character of each candidate was also assessed from the annual reports of his superiors. It was

in these reports that class and regional influences exerted themselves. As a result candidates of noble birth, or from families with strong military traditions or owning land or industries, were more strongly represented in the northern military districts, than in those of the south-west, with its more democratic traditions. In Bavaria officers from families with academic or civil-service associations predominated. These tendencies were, however, typical of the content of the officer corps as a whole, and did not reflect any special bias in the General Staff. Here, if any single factor predominated, it was excellence in the performance of military duties.

The process of selection extended throughout the three years of training. The second year course usually followed the first without an examination, but the trainees were assessed by means of staff exercises on the autumn manoeuvres. At the end of the second year they were tested on a staff selection exercise (*Auswahlreise*). The candidates' performances and their records over the previous two years were then reassessed. Of approximately seventy, only some fifteen went on to the third year's 'R' course in the Reichswehr Ministry, Berlin. This took place for the first time in October 1923 under the direction of the Chief of the *Truppenamt*. The course was frequently visited by Seeckt, who took a close interest in the standards of instruction and the performance and character of each trainee. The third year also ended with a two week tactical field exercise. The majority (eight or ten) passed, because, as Hansgeorg Model states in his study on the subject, by then 'the wheat had been sorted from the chaff'.

The objective of the programme was 'to train assistants for the senior field commanders and the central command structure, and to produce officers qualified to be advisers, assistants and executors of their leaders' decisions'. The curriculum was much broader in scope then in the prewar *Kriegsakademie*. Seeckt insisted on the inclusion of more academic content. Nevertheless, General von Geyr later remarked that tactics was still studied with 'an almost religious fervour.' General Wilhelm Speidel described its purposes as: 'education towards that balanced, logical, tactical thinking which is the prerequisite to the appreciation of a tactical situation and for the evaluation of the relevant courses open; training towards ability in decision making, flexibility and clarity of thought, and stability of character in the face of the vicissitudes of the leadership; training in the swift, clear and careful issuing of orders . . .' As in the Imperial Army, stress was laid upon the basic principle of leaving the commander and his staff freedom in the choice of method and means for the achievement of the task allocated to them. However, the means available in most tactical situations confronting the Reichswehr were limited because of the absence of heavy weapons, reserves or air support. Sustained attack was out of the question and so the delaying battle (*hinhaltenden Kampf*) became the basis for many tactical studies.

The subjects taught on the first and second years of training consisted of tactics, military history, army organisation, army supply, arms instruction, signals, and air operations. Individual lectures were also given on the military intelligence service, the transportation services, the medical and veterinary services, and naval tactics. The third year's training comprised tactics, military history, general staff duties, army organisation, leadership and organisation in foreign armies, military intelligence, army supply, transportation services, army technical services, naval strategy, air defence, internal and external affairs of state, the economic situation, foreign languages and sports. The instructors for the first two years were selected from the divisional staff in each Military District. Those for the third year were senior general staff officers with war experience supported by specialists from the Reichswehr Ministry. Among the instructors on the staff courses were many officers who rose to high rank in the Second World War, including Field-Marshals List, Kluge, Manstein, Paulus, and Model, and Colonel-Generals Halder, Guderian, Jodl and Reinhardt. Manstein recalled in his memoirs that instructing the potential staff officers was an 'unusually gratifying task' because, with the small class of only eight students, it was possible to discuss problems in great detail. He felt that he probably learnt more than his pupils as a result of this experience. The staff courses conducted by the Reichswehr between 1923 and 1933 were of great importance to the future Wehrmacht because many staff majors and colonels holding posts of great importance and responsibility were trained in those difficult years. However, the restrictions of the Treaty of Versailles placed great limitations on the scope of staff training. There was no opportunity in Germany to study new developments in air warfare, the use of tanks, heavy artillery or chemical weapons. So in addition to the staff training conducted within the structure of the Reichswehr the General Staff also developed a series of courses and exchanges with the Red Army.

General von Seeckt began to express his thoughts of the idea of working with Russia in January 1920. The defeat of the Soviet offensive against Poland in that year made the Russians eager for German help. The first move, in April 1921, was made in the field of economic co-operation. Significantly, the German negotiators were led by Major Oskar Ritter von Niedermayer, a retired general staff officer and close associate of Seeckt. As the contacts developed a 'Special Group R' was formed in the *Truppenamt* to handle the secret economic and military agreements. But the actual meetings with the Russians were conducted in the Berlin apartment of Colonel Kurt von Schleicher. In November 1922 the Minister of Defence gave orders that the Chief of the *Truppenamt*, General Otto Hasse, was to be responsible for co-ordinating all the projects in Russia. An office, '*Zentrale Moskau*', was set up in the Soviet capital, staffed by 'retired' general staff officers. Their task was to supervise the German personnel in Russian training centres or on attachment to Red Army units. Regular visits by senior officers were also arranged in order to build up a harmonious relationship between the two armies. Seeckt's main purpose in developing this military alliance was no less than the destruction of Poland

and restoration of Germany's eastern frontiers of 1914.

The establishment of armament industries and military training centres in Russia which resulted from the 'eastern policy' gave the Germans a small delusion of escape from the 'fetters of Versailles', but they were never developed to the scale required to make the Reichswehr capable of waging offensive war in the 1920s. At first the *Truppenamt* refused to face the truth. In 1923 General Hasse assured the Russians that Germany would wage a great War of Liberation in 'three to five years'. A year later Lieutenant-Colonel Joachim von Stülpnagel, Chief of the Operations Section of the *Truppenamt* called for a national military revival after the example of Prussia in 1813. In November 1924 the *Rüstungsamt* (Armament Office) was established to plan the military-economic aspects of such a

Soviet officers attend staff training centres of the German Reichswehr

President Hindenburg motors through the streets of Cologne with the city's Burgomaster Dr Adenauer

revival. But in the following year a change took place which curtailed the aggressive ambitions of the Reichswehr.

On 26th April 1925 the old *Feldherr*, Field-Marshal Paul von Hindenburg, was elected President. This event narrowed the gulf between the army and the State and reduced both the independence of the Reichswehr and the stature of its Chief. The new President had no liking for the person or policies of Seeckt. He shared the doubts of those who thought that 'the Sphinx' had overplayed his eastern policy when he opposed Stresemann's efforts in the West. Though Hindenburg did not openly condemn Seeckt,

Seeckt is replaced by General Heye

the old man's critical attitude and his prestige in the army gave encouragement to the grumbling opposition of the arrogant general. Otto Gessler, the Reichswehr Minister, gained new courage, and within eighteen months of Hindenburg's election, he took advantage of a political slip on the part of the Chief of Army Direction to force him to resign.

Seeckt was succeeded by General Wilhelm Heye, a commoner who was regarded with some condescension by the general staff corps. Like a benevolent sergeant-major, 'Onkel Heye' was popular with the rank and file. But under his leadership the power and influence of the Reichswehr passed from the *Heeresleitung* (Army High Command) to the general staff officers in the Reichswehr Ministry who grouped themselves round the controversial person of General Kurt von Schleicher. As a subaltern in the Third Regiment of Foot Guards, Schleicher had cultivated the friendship of Oskar von Hindenburg, son of the Field-Marshal. Access to the President's home gave Schleicher opportunities which he exploited to the full. This, however, was not his only avenue of approach. His ability at the *Kriegsakademie* had caught the attention of the First Quartermaster-General, General Gröner, who had appointed him as his adjutant. Later, he served in the *Truppenamt* under Hasse, and in 1926 became head of the newly established *Wehrmachtabteilung*, the Armed Forces Section, in the Reichswehr Ministry. This section combined the political liaison element of the *Truppenamt* with the military *Adjutantur* of the Reichswehr Minister, and added financial, legal, intelligence and public relations offices to form a most important organisation. It dealt with both army and naval matters, thus it formed the first nucleus of a general staff for the combined services. Growing into the Ministerial Office and then the Wehrmacht Office, in the hands of Blomberg, Reichenau and Keitel it was later to swallow up its parent body, the War Ministry, and emerge as the High Command of the Wehrmacht, a combined services staff rivalling the Army General Staff. While the men in the *Wehrmachtabteilung* were more interested in politics than tactics, the great majority of general staff officers confined themselves to military technology and regarded Schleicher and his adherents with some distaste and embarrassment.

A further effect of Seeckt's departure upon the general staff corps was reflected in the memorandum written by Lieutenant-Colonel von Bonin, Chief of the Organisation Section of the *Truppenamt*. This advocated a reduction in illegal activities which damaged the efforts of the government to win Germany a position of trust in her relations with the nations of Western Europe. Nevertheless, the co-operation with Russia continued because it was regarded as too important to be abandoned. The number of German officers who gained technical or staff training in Russia was small. The best results were obtained at the flying training school at Lipetsk where about 120 fighter pilots and a hundred observers were trained between 1925 and 1933. Staff officers of the *Fliegerzentrale* secretly maintained within the *Truppenamt* also received training in Russia, including many like Sperrle, Jeschonnek and Student who later rose to positions of importance in the Luftwaffe. The chemical warfare school at Volsk and the tank school at Kazan only came into full operation in 1929. The latter had only one instructor and ten officer students from the Reichswehr. However, experiments with German and British tanks there led to the development of the Panzers Mark III and Mark IV which were the backbone of the German armoured forces in the Second World War. The visits conducted to Red Army training centres and attendance at manoeuvres were also of great importance to the German general staff corps. The officers on such visits were amazed at the Russians' readiness to show them everything they wanted to see. As a result they gained insight into the serious lack of initiative and responsibility at the lower levels of command, and the rigidity of the Russians' operations and tactics.

At the beginning of the thirties the Reichswehr consisted of only 21 infantry and 3 cavalry divisions

What the Germans learnt served them ill in the long run because too many were convinced that the Red Army was incapable of becoming battleworthy. Between 1927 and 1933 the visiting groups included senior members of the general staff including Blomberg, Heye, Hammerstein, and Adam. But among the more junior visitors were many names which were to win prominence in the Wehrmacht: Brauchitsch, Keitel, Hoth, Jeschonnek and Manstein.

By the time he went to Russia with General Adam in 1931, Manstein had already won an outstanding reputation in the General Staff. A tall, distinguished Prussian, he had served with distinction in the 3rd Foot Guards, and on divisional army and army group staffs in the First World War. On 1st September 1929 he became head of Group One in Section T1 (Operations) of the *Truppenamt*, and began the process of expansion which prepared the German Army for the Second World War exactly ten years later. He rejected the proposals of the Organisation Section (T2) which envisaged the expansion of the army to three cavalry and sixteen infantry divisions, by forming nine new infantry divisions, eight of which would be armed with weapons sent from 'somewhere abroad after the outbreak of war'. Manstein was sceptical and regarded these unarmed divisions as merely 'a means of increasing the number of prisoners-of-war in the hands of the enemy'. Instead he suggested that the Reichswehr should triple itself from within. The Reichswehr had been trained so that every officer, NCO and man could fill the job of his immediate superior. Thus, argued Manstein, on the mobilization of reservists and volunteers each subunit, unit and formation should absorb the new arrivals. Each infantry section would become a platoon, each platoon a company, each company a battalion, and so on until the seven peace-time divisions expanded into twenty-one. Quality would be

maintained by the presence of the cadre of regulars forming a third of each unit. The three cavalry divisions were sufficient, so all reserves of horses, weapons and equipment could go to the infantry divisions. Nevertheless, a ruthless reconstruction of every unit's war establishment was necessary to find weapons. Only combat soldiers carried rifles. Signallers, engineers, etc. had at most a pistol. The number of light MGs in each company was reduced from nine to six. The heavy MGs in the battalion were cut from twelve to six. The artillery battery was reduced from four to three guns.

Manstein's plan resulted in changes in the entire organisation, tactics, training and mobilization of the Army. It was a mighty undertaking for a major, even a general staff major. But Manstein was not a man who stood in awe of the high command. According to General Westphal, 'he was always charming to subordinates . . . [but] intolerably arrogant with his equals and superiors.' Colonel Geyer, Head of T1 was inclined to be very critical but he could not fault the logic of Manstein's proposals. Fortunately for the young major, the *Truppenamt* had a new chief, General Wilhelm Adam, a lively, open minded Bavarian who liked quick decisions. He immediately accepted Manstein's plan, and soon won over the Chief of Army Direction, General von Hammerstein, who had never been happy about forming eight unarmed divisions. Not everyone was pleased, however, at Manstein's success. The Organisation Section, 'which now had to throw all their work in the fire and . . . produce a new plan', was 'not exactly enthusiastic'. Unfortunately for von Manstein the head of this section was an unimaginative but industrious man with a penchant for institutional politics. Such a man was dangerous to cross. His name was Wilhelm Keitel.

The next major problem handled by the energetic Major von Manstein

General Wilhelm Adam

General Hammerstein

was that of how the Reichswehr would respond to an attack on Germany. 'This,' he wrote, 'is surely the most important and interesting task which can confront a soldier . . . But . . . how should we develop plans . . . in view of the overwhelming superiority of the three neighbours allied against Germany?' France had 30 regular divisions, Poland 25 and several cavalry brigades, and Czechoslovakia 15 plus cavalry. France could triple, and her allies could double their forces after mobilization. Under these circumstances it was impossible to draw up a firm, inflexible deployment plan (*Aufmarschplan*). In any case, after the bitter experiences of 1914 such a plan was not considered desirable. The Reichswehr, even when expanded to 21 infantry and 3 cavalry divisions, was so small that the railways could move it quickly in any direction at short notice. As a result no Defensive Concentration Plan was developed by the German General Staff until 1937. However, in East Prussia the Frontier Defence Forces (*Grenzschutzverbände*) were too weak to engaged in mobile warfare so a defensive redoubt, the 'Heilsberger Triangle', was con-

structed of barbed wire entanglements, anti-tank obstacles, and small concrete bunkers. In order to ensure a swift decision-making process in the event of a war the Operations Section worked out a great number of possible situations and practiced the reactions of the higher formation commanders and staffs in a series of war games and staff journeys (*Übungsreisen*). The purpose of these journeys was to develop and practice the uniform exercise of command over large formations, to become familiar with all those areas of Germany which might become theatres of operations, and to enable all participants to become personally acquainted with one another and thus to foster close co-operation and understanding. This helped to make the German General Staff a formidable military instrument in the Second World War. The bonds of mutual confidence between commanders and staff officers also helped them to stand the strains which political crises and sudden expansion placed upon the army's command structure in the first years of Hitler's rule.

Expansion

As soon as he came to power Hitler told his (Reichswehr) Minister, Blomberg, that he wished to meet the leaders of the armed forces. Since the Military District Commanders were coming to Berlin for a conference on 3rd February Blomberg arranged a dinner that evening at the apartment of General von Hammerstein. The señor admirals, the Foreign Minister, Neurath, and Hitler were also invited. After they had eaten, Hitler rose and outlined his policy. The overall aim, he said, was to win political power. Internally there must be a rooting out of all opposition, pacifism, marxism, and 'the cancer of democracy'. Physical fitness must be fostered in the young and a 'warlike spirit' revived in the whole people. External policy must be directed against the Treaty of Versailles. The economic problems could only be solved by drastic means because Germany's living space was too restricted. Conscription had to return, because the build up of the armed forces was the most important prerequisite to regaining political power. 'When it is won, how shall this power be used? Now it is too early to say. Perhaps for winning new export possibilities, or perhaps – and indeed better – for the conquest of living space in the East and its ruthless Germanisation.' The internal struggle was not the affair of the armed forces. They should concentrate on rearmament, for this will be a most dangerous period during which 'it will be seen if France has any statesmen; if so she will leave us no time, but fall upon us (possibly with eastern satellites).'

Most of the generals regarded Hitler's speech as a cheap attempt to win their support with promises of military expansion. Nevertheless, the danger of a violent reaction by France or Poland or both was real enough to alarm Generals von Fritsch and Fromm. The Chief of the *Truppenamt,* General Adam shared their concern, and a month later, when the Poles started to reinforce their garrison at the fortress of Westerplatte near Danzig, he stated that 'We cannot at the moment prosecute a war. We must do everything to avoid one even at the cost of a diplomatic defeat'.

In October 1933 General Ludwig Beck became Chief of the *Truppenamt.* Beck was a far more cautious man than General Adam and he not only shared his predecessor's anxiety about the political situation, but questioned the military effectiveness of von Manstein's plan to triple the army. However, at the time he took office one battalion of Infantry Regiment 9 was expanded to form a new regiment. It was then tried out in an exercise against two battalions from Potsdam with encouragingly good results. So in January 1934 the *Truppenamt* sent out orders to the staffs of the Military Districts to begin the process of trebling the army. Almost immediately their plans were thrown into confusion by the order that all formations must supply suitable personnel, including 200 officers, for the new Luftwaffe.

The decision to develop the air force as a separate service was probably the result of Hermann Göring's ambition. As the man second only to Hitler in the Party and State, the former captain and 'ace' of the Imperial Air Service was determined to make the new air force a personal creation, and had no intention of allowing it to remain as parts of the army and navy. Thus many officers who had secretly worked for years to develop the air arms of their services were obliged to don a new uniform and join Erhard Milch and administrators from the *Lufthansa* and Göring's col-

lection of old comrades from the squadrons of the First World War. Göring's rank rose from captain to general, and Lörzer, Bodenschatz, Udet, Greim, Schleich, Keller and Christiansen became colonels overnight. Many of them proved to be capable commanders, but the bulk of the Luftwaffe high command was taken from the ranks of the General Staff of the Army. Some, like Wilberg, Wachenfeld, Kaupitsch, Halm, Schweickhard and Volkmann, never achieved distinction. But Kesselring, Sperrle, Stumpff, Student, and Richthofen rose to commanding positions in the war. General Wever, the first Chief of the Luftwaffe Staff, was killed in an air crash in 1935. He and his successors, Kesselring, Stumpff, and Jeschonnek, were all former members, of the general staff of the army. Wever was an advocate of the strategic heavy bomber but his successors thought of the air force mainly as a supporting service for the Army. Their influence was reflected in the Luftwaffe's equipment and tactics, which were designed primarily for winning air superiority over the battlefield and supporting the ground forces. Nevertheless, Göring's ambitions for himself and his air force

Left to right: Blomberg, Hitler, Generals Beck and Bock during manoeuvres of a transport division

seriously weakened the general staff's attempts to make the army *primus inter pares* in the exercise of high command in war. Instead a strong case began to develop for the creation of a Wehrmacht staff exercising command over all three services.

At first the general staff did not fully appreciate the danger of a division in its ranks. Until the summer of 1934 it was preoccupied by the rivalry of the *Sturmabteilung*, the storm troop army of the Nazi Party, which had grown to a force of two and a half million men. The Chief of Staff of the SA, Ernst Röhm, a former army captain, regarded the generals as 'a lot of old fogeys' and was horrified that Hitler should turn to these 'reaction-

aries' and not to his new, 'revolutionary' army. As it became clear that Hitler placed greater reliance upon the professional skill of the Reichswehr than upon the élan of the 'brown battalions', Röhm began to talk recklessly about a 'second revolution'. On 28th February 1934, the anniversary of Field-Marshal Graf von Schlieffen's birth, the members of the *Verein Graf Schlieffen*, the Association of General Staff Officers, gathered in Berlin as usual for their annual dinner. Hitler decided to take advantage of the presence of so many senior generals to summon them, together with the leaders of the SA and SS, to hear his views on the roles of their respective organisations. He stated that the present measures to bring economic relief could last only for about eight years. After that there would be 'frightful destitution'. Living space

Ernst Röhm, leader of the SA

would have to be gained, but the Western Powers would try to prevent this. 'Therefore, short, decisive blows to the West and then to the East could be necessary.' Military history showed that a militia, like the SA, would not be suitable. The hastily trained reserve division in which he had served in 1914 had suffered severely at Langemarck. Therefore the people's army must be built up on the Reichswehr and rigorously trained in order to be ready for defence in five years and for attack after eight years. During the initial period of rearmament the SA might assist with frontier defence and pre-military training but 'the Wehrmacht must be the only bearer of arms of the nation'.

Röhm, however, refused to accept the judgement of the 'ignorant corporal', as he called Hitler. Finally, as is well known, the Führer decided to purge the Party of the dangerous elements in the SA leadership. He took the opportunity to kill off a number of other political enemies including the former Chancellor General Kurt von Schleicher and Major-General von Bredow, who had succeeded Schleicher as Head of the Ministerial Office. The members of the general staff corps were shocked at the cold-blooded murder of their former comrades. Many had been embarrassed by their intrigues and felt that they should 'never have delved so deeply into a mucky business like politics'. But their deaths could not simply be overlooked. In spite of Blomberg's order forbidding discussion of the matter Field-Marshal von Mackensen spoke up at the annual dinner of the *Verein Graf Schlieffen* in February 1935 and stated that Schleicher and Bredow had 'died in all honour'. Shortly after the killings Mackensen had also sent a protest to President von Hindenburg, but by this time the old man was dying.

Anticipating the death of the President, the officer who was now sitting at Schleicher's former desk in the *Wehrmachtamt*, Major-General Walter von Reichenau, was busy composing a new oath of loyalty. When it was issued its wording inflicted a further shock on the officer corps, for it was not to the State nor to the constitution but to the person of Adolf Hitler that loyalty was to be pledged. The new oath was issued on 2nd August 1934, a day which General Beck described as 'the blackest' of his life. Disturbed as it was by these events, the general staff had little time to reflect upon them. It was immersed in a period of intense work.

By the autumn of 1934 the *Truppenamt* was in the process of tripling the infantry divisions. On 1st October the strength of the Reichswehr reached 240,000 volunteers. Meanwhile, secret plans were made for the reintroduction of conscription and a further expansion to twelve corps each of three divisions. When Hitler announced this in March 1935 many of the commanding generals were taken by surprise and even critical at the sudden strains 'imposed by such a rapid expansion. In May 1935 the Defence Law was published. In addition to details of the conscription programme it contained a new nomenclature for the high command. The Reichswehr Minister became War Minister, the Chief of Army Direction was now Commander-in-Chief of the Army and the *Truppenamt* was called what it always had been, the General Staff of the Army. But mere titles were not enough. The substance also had to be revived. The tiny force of staff officers trained in the Reichswehr now had to be expanded to meet the needs of the massive Wehrmacht demanded by Hitler. Nevertheless, no lowering of standards was permitted in the preparatory training for the staff examination, nor in the week-long examination itself. In 1936, for instance, about a thousand officers assembled at the seven *Wehrkreis* (Military District) headquarters to take the exam; of these only about 150 entered the *Kriegsakademie*. However, in order to increase the output of the academy between 1933 and 1937 the course was reduced from three to two years. This resulted in a concentration upon purely military subjects and drastic reductions in the broader areas of economics and politics. The course began on 1st October with nine months of lectures interspersed with staff exercises, and the weekly field exercise without troops. At the end of the following June the students were sent for a three-month tour of duty with an arm of the service other than their own. Then they took part in the autumn manoeuvres and, on 1st October, commenced their second year which followed a similar pattern. The instructors were headed by the Commandant (General Curt Liebmann, 1935-April 1939; General Eugen Müller, April – August 1939). Each annual intake was directed by a colonel of the general staff, aided by several tactics instructors most of whom were senior, active staff officers with long experience on divisional staffs.

The primary aim of the *Kriegsakademie* was to train general staff officers as advisers and assistants to formation commanders or as members of the central command apparatus of the OKH. The course was not designed to train future senior commanders nor to provide staff officers for Wehrmacht (inter-service or ministerial) appointments. While General Adam was Chief of the *Truppenamt* the instruction encouraged the students to study operational as well as tactical problems. But when General Beck took his place the training was restricted to the framework of the division and all operational studies involving the deployment and command of higher formations were forbidden. Typically, Beck fixed his eye upon the immediate, pressing need of the expanding army, and preferred to leave the broader aspects of operational training for special senior officers' courses. However, many staff officers, including Hermann Förtsch, who was a tactics instructor between 1936 and 1938, felt in retrospect that Beck was mistaken in imposing such narrow limits on staff training. The rapid expansions of the Wehrmacht meant that many staff officers served only for a few months in divisional staffs before being sent on to higher formation headquarters where they felt the lack of training in dealing with operational problems. The third year of training, which was reintroduced in 1937, brought a partial improvement. Though the stress remained on the division, the command problems of the corps and occasionally the army were now given some study. Beck was also criticised for stopping Adam's practice of allowing the students rather than the instructor to set tactical problems for their comrades. While restoring a highest degree of 'consistency and steadiness', Beck's methods made the instruction more prosaic and less challenging. The same characteristics resulted from the rigid practice of basing all the tactics instruction upon 'infantry units marching on foot'. As a result 'there was no room for the presentation of experiences in the command and supplying of large

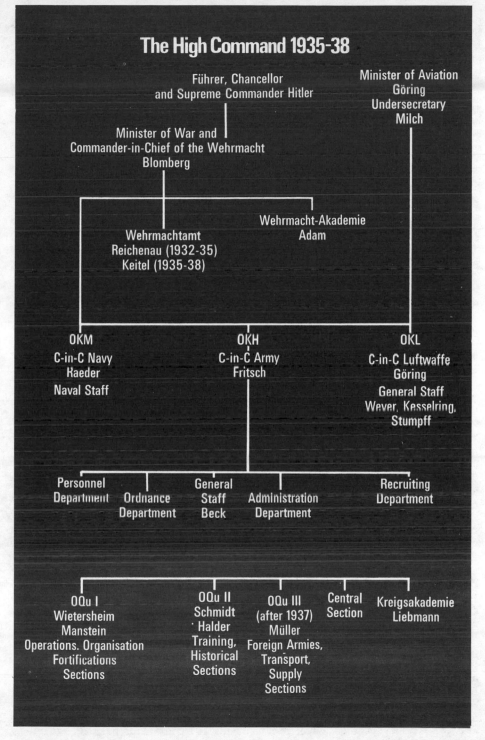

The High Command 1935-38

Führer, Chancellor and Supreme Commander Hitler

Minister of Aviation Göring Undersecretary Milch

Minister of War and Commander-in-Chief of the Wehrmacht Blomberg

Wehrmacht-Akademie Adam

Wehrmachtamt Reichenau (1932-35) Keitel (1935-38)

OKM C-in-C Navy Raeder Naval Staff

OKH C-in-C Army Fritsch

OKL C-in-C Luftwaffe Göring General Staff Wever, Kesselring, Stumpff

Personnel Department

Ordnance Department

General Staff Beck

Administration Department

Recruiting Department

OQu I Wietersheim Manstein Operations, Organisation Fortifications Sections

OQu II Schmidt Halder Training, Historical Sections

OQu III (after 1937) Müller Foreign Armies, Transport, Supply Sections

Central Section

Kreigsakademie Liebmann

Schleicher and Bredow were among
those killed during the purge

motorized formations. The ideas
about a . . . war of movement pro-
pagated by General Guderian and
the new Panzer troops . . . hardly pene-
trated the *Kriegsakademie* before the
outbreak of the Second World War'.
Similarly, the tactical and operational potential of air support was
entirely neglected. The Luftwaffe,
jealously guarding its independence
as a service, made little attempt to
exchange ideas on staff training with
the army. Thus in the teachings of the
Kriegsakademie the tactical contribution of the Luftwaffe was limited to
air reconnaissance.

Considering the limitations of the
tactical and operational instruction
in the *Kriegsakademie* how can the
remarkable military successes of the
Blitzkrieg campaigns be explained?
Of course, it must be remembered that
the full measure of co-operation between land and air forces, and co-
ordination of arms which character
ized the Blitzkrieg in France was
achieved only after the Wehrmacht
had carried out major 'dress rehear-
sals' in Austria and Czechoslovakia
and 'preliminary bouts' in Poland
and Norway. Nevertheless, several feat-

ures of the general staff training
compensated for the narrowness of
its tactical teaching. The speed and
efficiency of well-practiced staff pro-
cedures, which were uniform throughout the army, helped to ensure clear,
concise orders and correct responses.
The very frequent tactical rides, staff
journeys, and field exercises without
troops resulted in skilled map reading
and that accurate perception of
terrain which is essential to successful
tactics. Furthermore, contrary to
popular myth, the German army was
not rigid in its tactics and operations.
According to General Langhaeuser,
'It was a basic principle that there
were no "patented solutions"; every
well considered and well founded view-
point could be accepted'. Commanders
and their staffs were encouraged to be
flexible and imaginative in their
appreciation of the situation and in
the plan resulting from it.

Some compensation for the narrowness of the tactical training was also
provided by the military history programme which was second only to
tactics in importance on the curriculum. The instructors were retired staff
officers, mostly generals, and were
permanently on the faculty of the
academy. General von der Groeben
recalled that their greater age made

General Reichenau composed the new oath of loyalty to Adolf Hitler

Military Sciences, founded by General von Cochenhausen. Foreign language classes were voluntary, but well attended. Riding and physical training were included in the curriculum to ensure that all students kept fit. According the General Berendsen, the qualities sought, in addition to military competence and knowledge, included 'quick mental perception, the ability to think logically, swiftness in decision making, insight for essentials and for coherence, the ability to be creative and not cling to regulations, and the ability to work reliably for long periods without tiring'.

In his study of the general staff officer's training Hansgeorg Model concludes that the curriculum of the *Kriegsakademie* should have included more instruction on modern developments, especially '. . . the complexities of supply, motorisation and operational employment of Panzer formations, co-operation with the Luftwaffe, war economy, military technology and, not least, the handling of political questions'.

Students were assessed by their tactics instructor throughout the course. Thus there was no need for a final exam. However, borderline cases were closely watched by the senior instructors and the commandant on the fourteen-day Final Field Exercise (*Schlussreise*). Candidates who did not qualify for general staff appointments were usually sent to the War Ministry, or became senior adjutants or tactics instructors in military schools. Those who qualified went on a probationary period of up to eighteen months in a general staff appointment. When this was successfully completed the candidates could don silver collar patches, and carmine stripes on their breeches, and place the letters iG (*im Generalstab*) after their rank.

them somewhat remote from their students and their instruction was often rather dry and unimaginative. According to Berendsen and Teske they gave excessive details of military deployments, battles and engagements, but neglected 'the broad interrelationship between policy, economics and strategy' in which the most valuable lessons of military history are to be found. Nevertheless, according to General Langhaeuser, topics were selected which contained some parallels with the situation in Germany as seen by her soldiers in the 1930s. 'So we were lectured on the campaigns of the improvised (republican) army of the French Revolutionary War or of the American Civil War. By this means the principles of strategic defence were . . . presented.'

The other subjects taught included supply and transport, motorisation, the supporting arms and technical services, and war economy. Special lectures were also given on espionage, military intelligence, and foreign armies. Evening lectures on politics, history, economics and geopolitics were sponsored by groups such as the German Society for Strategic and

Before 1933 only about one third of the trainees qualified for general staff appointments, but to meet the needs of Hitler's expansion of the Army in the 1930s two thirds were recommended. This annual output, the

The oath of total obedience to the Führer

reduction of the course to two years for most candidates between 1935 and 1937, and an increased annual intake: (1932–43, 1933–63, 1934–88, 1935–136, 1936–100 all on two-year programmes; 1937–150, July 1938–39 Austrian officers, October 1938–140, 1939–216) helped to meet the need for junior staff officers. But the greatest problem between 1935 and 1938 was to fill appointments with staff majors and colonels. In 1934 the General Staff had estimated the army's need in 1937 at 246 staff officers. However, as Hitler stepped up his demands for expansion the actual number of general staff appointments in 1937 was 545 (high command – 105, formation HQs – 387, Führer reserve – 20, liaison officers at army and corps HQs – 33). To find 300 extra staff officers the following measures were adopted: the reduction of staff officers' tours of duty in non-staff appointments; changes in the limits on age and rank for certain staff appointments; employing

officers who failed to qualify at the *Kriegsakademie* (this was only done after the outbreak of war); the elimination of some less important staff jobs; the recalling of former general staff officers for employment on mobilization, especially in the Reserve Army; the take-over of staff officers and the Senior Officers Course of the Austrian Federal Army (of 92 active staff officers available, 15 colonels, 8 lieutenant-colonels, and 8 captains were transferred to the German General Staff); a special course at the *Kriegsakademie* in July 1938 for 39 Austrian candidates. As a result of these measures by September 1939 the General Staff had 415 fully trained staff officers, 93 officers re-called or transferred to the General Staff, and 303 general staff candidates at the *Kriegsakademie* or on probation; a total of 811 officers. Since on mobilization there were 824 appointments to be filled, it was necessary to close down the *Kriegsakademie* at the outbreak of war and employ all candidates in staff appointments. Thus the German general staff corps entered the Second World War with its resources already overstretched.

The majority of general staff officers were sent to a formation headquarters for their probationary period. The headquarters of army groups, armies, corps and divisions were divided into three sections. In the command section the general staff officer Ia was responsible for operational and tactical command, organisation and training, and the Ic dealt with reconnaissance, intelligence, counter espionage and morale. In the quartermaster's section, the divisional general staff officer Ib or army *Oberquartiermeister* directed supplies, transportation, and the administration of the combat zone. In the army group and corps headquarters the quartermaster's section was kept small to leave the staff free to concentrate upon operational and tactical direction. The third section was the *Adjutantur* in which the IIa managed all personnel administration and legal and religious matters.

Army group, army and corps commanders were served by a chief of staff, a senior general staff officer who acted as chief adviser and planner. In the absence of the commander the chief of staff was authorized to make decisions and issue orders. In addition to his reponsibilities to his commander, a chief of staff was also responsible to the chief of staff of the next higher formation and ultimately to the Chief of the General Staff of the army for all matters relating to the training, assessment and appointment of the general staff officers in his formation.

Some of the most able officers were sent straight from the *Kriegsakademie* to one of the departments of the High Command of the Army (OKH). The most sought-after were the appointments on the General Staff of the army. Before 1935 the *Truppenamt* had consisted of five sections: T1 – operations, T2 – organisation, T3 – enemy armies, T4 – training and T5 – transportation. By 1939 the General Staff had expanded into fourteen sections employing 85 general staff officers. These included five *Oberquartiermeister* who were appointed to relieve pressure on the Chief of the General Staff and to provide senior staff officers to become chiefs of staff of the army groups on mobilization.

The training of these very senior staff officers was conducted within the General Staff by means of wargames, staff journeys, annual manoeuvres. Each year every staff officer above the rank of major was given a problem on which to write a memorandum (*Denkschrift*) or study. However, the War Minister, Blomberg, was not satisfied that the problems of inter-service co-operation and grand strategy were adequately covered by such methods, and in 1935 he supported General von Reichenau's proposals for a *Wehrmacht-Akademie* to meet the need for training senior commanders and staff officers. To reconcile the Army General Staff to the new institution, von Reichenau suggested that General Adam, the former Chief of the *Truppenamt*, should become its first commandant. In his unpublished journal Adam describes the academy and its problems: 'My personal staff was small; it consisted of . . .: an admiral, a senior staff officer as chief of staff, and a naval officer as adjutant. There were also part-time instructors from all areas, officials from the ministries, diplomats, university professors, economics teachers, academics from various disciplines. I had the means to bring in men of special eminence, and each one felt honoured to be able to speak in our circle. Whenever one of our ambassadors was in Berlin he gave a lecture on the land to which he was accredited. Dr Schacht lectured and put his best associates at our disposal, thus we obtained rare insight into industry, banking, economics etc. I set aside one day each week for the preparation of my own lectures.

The OKH 1938-39

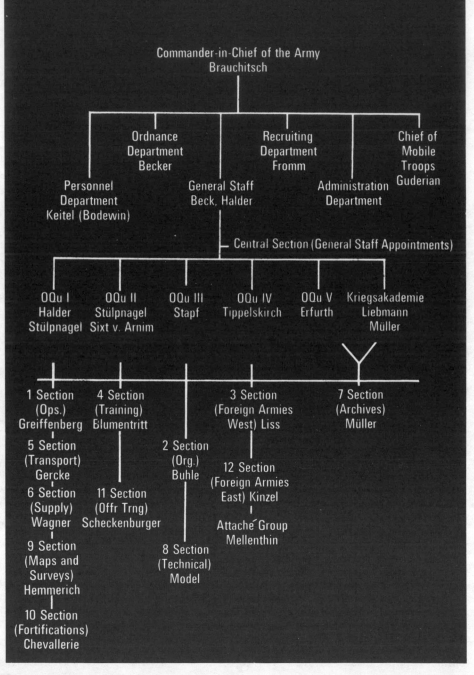

Commander-in-Chief of the Army
Brauchitsch

Ordnance
Department
Becker

Recruiting
Department
Fromm

Chief of
Mobile
Troops
Guderian

Personnel
Department
Keitel (Bodewin)

General Staff
Beck, Halder

Administration
Department

Central Section (General Staff Appointments)

OQu I
Halder
Stülpnagel

OQu II
Stülpnagel
Sixt v. Arnim

OQu III
Stapf

OQu IV
Tippelskirch

OQu V
Erfurth

Kriegsakademie
Liebmann
Müller

1 Section
(Ops.)
Greiffenberg

4 Section
(Training)
Blumentritt

3 Section
(Foreign Armies
West) Liss

7 Section
(Archives)
Müller

5 Section
(Transport)
Gercke

2 Section
(Org.)
Buhle

12 Section
(Foreign Armies
East) Kinzel

6 Section
(Supply)
Wagner

11 Section
(Offr Trng)
Scheckenburger

Attaché Group
Mellenthin

9 Section
(Maps and
Surveys)
Hemmerich

8 Section
(Technical)
Model

10 Section
(Fortifications)
Chevallerie

The OKW 1938-42

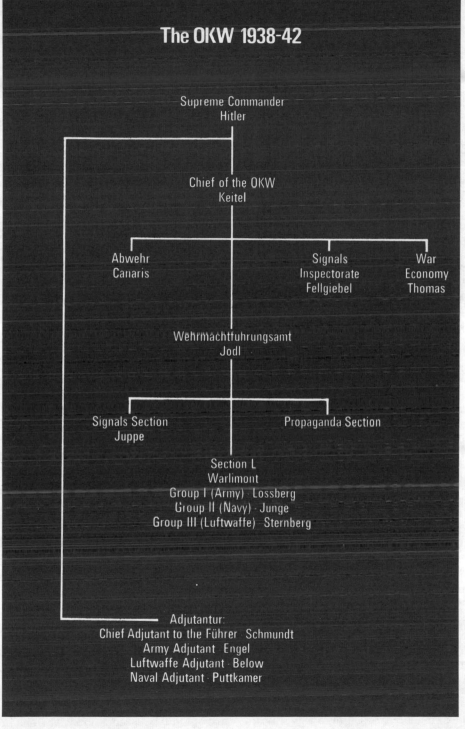

Supreme Commander
Hitler

Chief of the OKW
Keitel

Abwehr
Canaris

Signals
Inspectorate
Fellgiebel

War
Economy
Thomas

Wehrmachtfuhrungsamt
Jodl

Signals Section
Juppe

Propaganda Section

Section L
Warlimont
Group I (Army) - Lossberg
Group II (Navy) - Junge
Group III (Luftwaffe) - Sternberg

Adjutantur:
Chief Adjutant to the Führer - Schmundt
Army Adjutant - Engel
Luftwaffe Adjutant - Below
Naval Adjutant - Puttkamer

The Reichs Government reintroduces conscription in March 1935

These came under the general title "Strategy" (*Kriegsführung*). I demonstrated the relationship between policy and strategy and stressed the preeminence of policy. I cited leading statesmen and great captains and defined their areas of responsibility, pointing out that differences of opinion about ways and means were not harmful, but that uncertainty over basic aims ruled out hope of success. . . . We gave particular attention to the command structure and organisation . . . and the strategic value of armoured and air forces.' But in spite of all General Adam's efforts, the services, especially the Army and the Luftwaffe, regarded the *Wehrmacht-Akademie* as a threat to their independence, a step towards the establishment of a *Wehrmacht* general staff. As a result, Adam complained, 'Though I was supposed to get the best candidates for my courses, I often got the mediocre . . . Of my thirty students . . . only two got important jobs: one became Chief of Naval Staff,

and the other became Chief of Staff of the Luftwaffe (General Korten). In contrast to the military, the six most important ministries sent their best men as students.' Under these circumstances it was not possible for the academy to contribute to the development of a unified strategic doctrine for the Wehrmacht. Colonel-General Halder when questioned on this point after the war retorted that to expect such a contribution from the *Wehrmacht-Akademie* would be a 'grotesque overestimation of its importance'. Finally, Fritsch asked Blomberg to close the academy because the six senior general staff officers attending it were needed elsewhere. Adam felt that this request 'revealed the attitude of the army towards an institution which taught strategy', and decided to retire after the summer semester of 1938. In fact, the academy was disbanded in February shortly after Blomberg's resignation. Looking back, General Erhardt, formerly OQuV on the General Staff, regretted this outcome, because 'an inter-service academy and a combined staff are obviously essential institutions in

The interest in mechanization shown by Blomberg, here inspecting British tanks with General Wavell, was not reflected in the curriculum at the *Kriegsakademie*

modern armed forces'

Throughout the Second World War the German High Command suffered from the serious rivalry between the *Oberkommando der Wehrmacht* (OKW), the High Command of the armed forces, and the *Oberkommando des Heeres* (OKH), the High Command of the army. Accounts of this problem usually describe the OKW as a staff of sychophants recruited by Hitler in order to keep the General Staff in a subordinate place. This, however, oversimplifies the situation. Both staffs were drawn from the ranks of the general staff corps, and the rivalry between them was not initially over the question of support for Hitler's policies, but over the problem of the control of the armed forces in war.

Traditionally, the army was the dominant service, not only because Germany was a land power but also because the nature of her growth and development had been determined

mainly by the military successes of the Prussian army. But the status won for the General Staff under Moltke the Elder, had been lost by his successors. General von Seeckt overplayed his attempt to dictate policy, and his fall split the general staff corps. The majority kept out of politics and devoted themselves to military questions. But a small group in the Reichswehr Ministry led by Schleicher built the *Wehrmachtamt* into an office of some importance in determining military policy. Schleicher's fall left this office available to Hitler's Reichswehr Minister, Blomberg.

Werner von Blomberg combined intelligence and energy with a boyish enthusiasm, even naiveté. Nevertheless, he rose through the general staff to become Chief of the *Truppenamt* in 1927, and by 1930 he was viewed as the most likely successor to Heye as Chief of Army Direction. This, however, did not suit Schleicher who saw in Blomberg a man likely to attempt to win back from the Reichswehr Ministry the power he had acquired since Seeckt's fall. Schleicher, there-

An armoured infantry carrier during manoeuvres

fore, simply saddled Blomberg with the responsibility for certain 'illegal border security measures'. This, however, was not enough to force him out of the army, and Blomberg went off to East Prussia as commander of *Wehrkreis* I to await his chance for revenge. It came in January 1933 when Schleicher, now Chancellor, found himself bereft of all support and incapable of governing. Blomberg went to President Hindenburg and recommended a National Front Government under Hitler. Blomberg was rewarded with the post of Reichswehr Minister in Hitler's cabinet. Thus he not only got his revenge but did so by taking over Schleicher's role as the chief political general of the German army.

Blomberg's support for Hitler was encouraged by a vigorous and ruthlessly ambitious general staff officer named Walter von Richenau, who was

his Chief of Staff in *Wehrkreis* I. Reichenau was one of the few active officers with whom Hitler had made contact before 1933. In 1932 the Nazi leader wrote to him outlining his policy and the role of the Reichswehr in terms very similar to those he used later when speaking to the generals. When von Blomberg went to the Reichswehr Ministry von Reichenau accompanied him and became Head of the Ministerial Office, the *Wehrmachtamt*. On Hammerstein's retirement both Hitler and Blomberg wanted Reichenau to succeed him as Chief of Army Direction. But Hindenberg flatly rejected Reichenau as too political and too inexperienced in higher command. The Chief of the Army Personnel Office, Major-General von Schwedler, advised Blomberg that the man most acceptable to the army was General Werner Freiherr von Fritsch. Even Blomberg was forced to agree.

The appointment of Fritsch sharpened the debate within the general staff on the organisation of the high command. General Beck insisted that the command of the armed forces in war should be exercised by the Commander-in-Chief of the army advised by the Chief of the General Staff of the army. The War Ministry should confine itself to administrative and liaison tasks co-ordinating the political and economic policies with those of the armed forces. This view was criticised on the grounds that the technical developments of the 20th century, and the emergence of the air force as a third service made it essential to have an 'Armed Forces General Staff' responsible for overall strategic direction leaving the Army General Staff free to concentrate upon the planning and control of land operations. This view was expressed by some members of the General Staff, like Colonel Friederich Fromm, Chief of the Defence Office, and Lieutenant-Colonel Georg von Sodenstern, the head of the Organisation Section. But its most vigorous advocate was Walther Reichenau. In a memorandum written three months after his failure to secure the post of Commander-in-Chief, Reichenau urged the creation of a Wehrmacht High Command including operations, organisation and intelligence branches. Blomberg naturally supported Reichenau, and took the first step

General Fritsch, the conservative Commander-in-Chief from 1934 to 1938

Hitler and Blomberg inspect defences in East Prussia

towards implementing his proposals by creating in the Reichswehr Ministry a small tri-service operational planning staff, the *Abteilung Landesverteidigung*, the Department of National Defence. Beck tried to retain some influence over the new staff by arranging that a capable and ambitious staff officer named Alfred Jodl should head it. Colonel Jodl, however, was soon converted into a devoted admirer of Hitler and a supporter of the formation of a Wehrmacht General Staff. But Reichenau did not benefit from this success. In 1935 he went off to command *Wehrkreis* VII, presumably better to fit himself for the post of Commander-in-Chief when von Fritsch's term of office was completed. His successor in the *Wehrmachtamt* was Wilhelm Keitel. Blomberg's new right-hand man shared his predecessor's attitudes both towards Nazism and the idea of a Wehrmacht General Staff, but he was neither as showy nor as openly ambitious as Reichenau. Nevertheless in the long run he proved far more dangerous to the unity of the General Staff.

The division of opinion in the general staff corps was, therefore, not based upon a simple assessment of merits of the arguments. Blomberg, Reichenau and Keitel, were regarded by many general staff officers as over-ambitious politicalopportunists. The prospect of concentrating broad powers in the hands of such men was a strong argument against their apparently logical proposals. Colonel Jodl was probably right when he remarked to von Manstein, 'The pity of it is that the stronger personalities are in the OKH. If Fritsch, Beck and yourself were in the OKW you would think differently'. Fritsch and Beck was certainly regarded with respect and loyalty by their colleagues, but in Blomberg's view the opposition of Beck to the creation of a Wehrmacht General Staff was due to a combination of personal ambition and hidebound traditionalism. To regard the position of the Chief of the General Staff as comparable to that held by Moltke or Schleiffen was, Blomberg said, a 'gross exaggeration . . . which no longer corresponded to the realities of the times.' Nevertheless, many general staff officers saw their chief as a true successor to Moltke in character, method, manner and philosophy. Manstein who worked closely with him, thought that Beck 'Like Moltke, embodied the refined spirit of the intellectual rather than the soldier,' He did nothing hastily, but 'before each decision considered the minutest pros and cons and never allowed himself to be distracted by wishful thinking.' However, Manstein admitted, his meticulous fairness in assessing both sides of every argument did give an impression of indecisiveness. Certainly, in the matter of the organisation of the high command he was not in a sufficiently strong position to take the initiative. This was especially so after 1936, when Blomberg was promoted to the rank of field-marshal and confirmed in his appointment as War Minister and Commander-in-Chief of the Wehrmacht. Tension rose that winter at the Wehrmacht war game designed to study the problems of exercising leadership in war-time. Blomberg, Keitel and Jodl unfolded their ideas before Hitler and the senior generals and admirals. As soon as Hitler left, von Fritsch lost his temper and told Keitel that his interpretation of the role of the OKH was unacceptable. But a year later there was still no staff capable of planning the combined Wehrmacht manoeuvres and the task fell to General Franz Halder and the Training Section of the General Staff of the army. Meanwhile, von Manstein, now back in the General Staff as *Oberquartiermeister* I, had spent his summer holiday writing a memorandum on the problem of the organisation of the high command in war time. The clarity of his argument prompted von Fritsch to reiterate the army's case to Blomberg. It was a delusion he wrote, to regard the army as only equal to the other two services because for Germany warfare could be decisive only on land. A Wehrmacht High Command must therefore devote most of its attention to the army's operations and would soon become involved in conflicts with the OKH. However, if the OKH planned the operations of all three services the Wehrmacht High Command would be able to concentrate on the organisation and administration of the national resources in war. Blomberg rejected von Fritsch's proposals, but the two men agreed that they would 'talk to each other more often than at present, if possible, weekly'. But their period of co-operation was shortlived. A few months later, in February 1938, both Blomberg and Fritsch had been removed from office and the high command restructured to meet Hitler's wishes.

When Hitler replaced the War Ministry with a new staff, the *Oberkommando der Wehrmacht* (OKW), the High Command of the Armed Forces, it appeared that the case for the Wehrmacht General Staff had triumphed. However, Hitler did not appoint a new Commander-in-Chief of the Armed Forces. He reserved the title of *Oberster Befehlshaber der Wehrmacht* for himself, and appointed a *Chef* or Chief of Staff to head the new OKW. After the war Blomberg told General Warlimont how Hitler had consulted him on the question of who should take this post. After rejecting several possibilities he asked 'What's the name of that general who's been working with you up to now?' Blomberg answered 'Oh, Keitel; there's no question of him; he's nothing but the man who runs my office.' Hitler immediately retorted: 'That's exactly the man I'm looking for.'

Keitel himself was at first completely unaware of the true nature of his new appointment. He had no regrets when General von Fritsch, who had been so critical of his views on the organisation of the high command, was forced out of office by a sordid plot engineered by the SS. But to Keitel's disgust, the new Commander-in-Chief, General von Brauchitsch, wrote a memorandum repeating the view of his predecessor that it was impossible to separate the operational leadership of the Wehrmacht from that of the Army. Keitel promptly sat down and wrote a long reply. In this document, 'War Leadership as an Organisational Problem,' and its appendix on 'the war of the future', Keitel made it clear that he envisaged the OKW co-ordinating the economic psychological and military resources of the nation for total war as advocated by General Ludendorff in his book *Der totale Krieg* which had been published three years earlier. Through the *Wehrmachtführungsamt,* an operational staff headed by General von Viebahn, the OKW would direct the military strategy of the three services. In peacetime strategic ideas would be developed through the teachings of the *Wehrmacht-Akade-*

mie. However, Keitel was still not aware that such ideas did not bear much relation to reality. Hitler's grand strategy was not based upon Ludendoff's concept of total war but upon a series of decisive, limited wars fought against isolated victims, placing the minimum strain upon German people and their resources. The German war economy had long been a jungle of conflicting responsibilities in which the Wehrmacht had met serious rivalry. Field-Marshal Göring as head of the Four Year Plan Organisation and Commander-in-Chief of the Luftwaffe was hardly likely to allow Keitel to give him orders. Propaganda was the jealously guarded province of Dr Goebbels. Furthermore, Keitel's image of the OKW at the centre of strategic planning had already been shattered during the events leading up to the *Anschluss.* Hitler deliberately by-passed the OKW and worked directly with Göring, the OKH and the field commanders. Unabashed by this treatment, Keitel took upon himself the servile task of trying to avert friction by concealing the warnings and criticisms which the army leaders asked him to convey to Hitler.

For a time the Chief of the OKW could doubtless attribute Hitler's strange methods to the fact that new command structure had not had time to establish itself before the Austrian crisis broke out. But subsequent events showed that Hitler had no intention of making the OKW into anything more than a military secretariat. Policy and grand strategic decisions were reserved by Hitler for himself. He summoned the Commanders-in-Chief of the three services to receive his verbal orders for the preparation of military plans resulting from these decisions. The General Staff of the army then worked out an operations plan and presented it to Hitler. Amended and approved by Hitler, this plan, together with those of the Luftwaffe and navy, was then edited by the *Wehrmachtführungsamt* into a War Directive which Hitler

signed and issued as confirmation of the plans already submitted. Apart from this task, the *Wehrmachtführungsamt* was, in Warlimont's words. 'confined to an ill-defined sphere of activity, floating between the intuitive political initiatives of the Dictator and their military consequences.' Even the *Wehrmacht-Akademie* was a miserable failure and, as described above, was disbanded in 1938. Thus, by degrees Keitel came to realise that the OKW was 'a vacuum which only gave the Führer his desired freedom of action and faced me with an impossible task . . . and problems which

General Keitel, Chief of the OKW, and General Brauchitsch, Commander-in-Chief of the Army, talk with the Secretary of State for Air, General Milch

were never solved because the institution for dealing with them had been rejected.' Nevertheless, Hitler's failure to develop the OKW into a Wehrmacht General Staff did not signify a victory for the General Staff of the Army. On the contrary, Ludwig Beck and his colleagues faced the events of 1938 in a mood of deep dismay.

Blumenkrieg

In July 1935 Colonel von Manstein returned to the General Staff as head of the Operations Department, and a few months later he began work on plans for the mobilisation of the army in response to a French attack with Czechoslovakian support (Case 'Red'). The danger of a French attack was recognised by Hitler when he first discussed rearmament with the generals. The threat was reduced in 1934 by the pact he made with Poland, but it could become real again if France decided to intervene on the Saar or Rhineland questions.

In 1935 the Saar plebiscite went in Germany's favour without incident, and in February 1936 Hitler suddenly decided to remilitarise the Rhineland. Blomberg, who was away at the Winter Olympics, was not informed until Hitler had conferred with Fritsch. Two weeks later Beck summoned all the group and corps chiefs of staff to a conference in Berlin. Only after the army had made its operational plans did Blomberg issue a confirming directive for *Winterübung* (Winter Exercise). Five days later, on 7th March three battalions marched across the Rhine. The rest of the army was held back to parry any French reaction. None occurred, but when the German military attachés in London telegraphed 'Situation grave. Fifty-fifty peace or war'. Blomberg began to panic and urged Hitler to withdraw the battalions. The incident served to confirm the doubts in the OKH about von Blomberg's capability as Wehrmacht Commander-in-Chief. Furthermore, the manner in which he had been used only to confirm plans already decided upon by the OKH after direct consultation with Hitler encouraged Fritsch, Beck and Manstein in their hope that the General Staff would again become the chief agency for military planning and the direction of operations.

In 1937 Case 'Red' was still the most important plan, but Blomberg ordered studies for other possible situations: war against France and Czechoslovakia with the main concentration against the latter (Case 'Green'); armed intervention in Austria (Special Case 'Otto'); a war with Britain, Poland, and Lithuania (Special Case 'Extension Red-Green');

and warlike involvement with Red Spain (Special Case 'Richard'). In fact the Luftwaffe had been involved in Spain since the opening of the Civil War when it sent transport aircraft to ferry General Franco's Moroccans to the mainland. Lieutenant-Colonel Walter Warlimont of the General Staff, was sent to Franco's headquarters as Wehrmacht Plenipotentiary Delegate. The Spanish Civil War has often been described as the testing period for the tactics of the Blitzkrieg. But in fact the OKH was against sending ground forces to Spain in their semi-trained state and could not afford to take experienced men away from the newly expanded formations. However, Hitler was anxious to support Franco, so in November 1936 the Luftwaffe sent the 'Condor Legion' comprising 6,500 men and several squadrons of aircraft. In the following months further Luftwaffe personnel and some special army units were added to bring the Legion's strength up to almost 20,000 men. Generals Sperrle, Volkmann, and Richthofen developed the techniques of giving air support to ground troops and added to the dread of the bomber by cruel, demonstrative attacks on towns like Guernica. Colonel von Thoma's tanks were less impressive, especially when they met the heavier and better armed Russian models. But Hitler's real aim was to support Franco just enough to ensure 'a continuation of the Civil War and a preservation of the tensions in the Mediterranean' which might involve France and Britain in a war with Italy and give Germany an opportunity for the expansion of her *Lebensraum*.

This purpose, which Hitler had expressed in *Mein Kampf* and in his speeches to the generals, was more clearly defined in the address which he delivered to Blomberg, Fritsch, Göring, Raeder, and Foreign Minister Neurath on 5th November 1937. Colonel Hossbach, Hitler's senior adjutant, who was also there, later wrote an account of the meeting. The 'first aim', Hitler said, 'must be . . . to conquer Czechoslovakia and Austria simultaneously'. This must occur by 1943–45, or sooner if an opportunity occurs because France is either paralysed by civil strife or involved in a

In February 1936 Hitler makes the decision to remilitarise the Rhineland

war against another state. The listeners reacted to the speech with a series of objections. Even Blomberg was dismayed, and supported Fritsch's doubt that a war with Italy could prevent France from aiding Czechoslovakia. But when the time came for action both Blomberg and Fritsch were out of office, and Austria alone was the victim.

The war of nerves against Austria was intensified after Chancellor Schuschnigg's visit to Germany in February 1938. Keitel and Admiral Canaris, Head of the *Abwehr*, managed to convince the Austrians that Hitler was undertaking serious military preparations against them. The rattled Schuschnigg decided to hold a plebiscite in which Austrians would be asked to vote in support of their independence. Hitler fearing that Schuschnigg's appeal would succeed, decided to intervene and conduct *Anschluss* by force.

On 9th March, Hitler summoned Göring, Reichenau and General von Schobert, Commander of *Wehrkreis* VII, to the Reichs Chancellery. The following morning he sent for Keitel. Jodl rushed after him, having snatched up Blomberg's directive of 1937 because it included 'Special Case Otto'. In fact it was of little use, so Keitel swallowed his pride and hurried to the Bendlerstrasse to ask Beck if the General Staff had any plans for a move against Austria. Beck, who had regarded Blomberg's directives as 'hypothetical' could offer nothing. The new army Commander-in-Chief, Brauchitsch, was away so he agreed to go to the Chancellery. Significantly, Beck insisted on making a detour to pick up his most valued assistant, Manstein. At this moment Manstein in fact was no longer OQuI. A few days earlier he had been ordered to take command of an infantry division in Silesia. This was one of the spate of changes in the OKH which had fol-

lowed the resignation of von Fritsch. Brauchitsch had no cause to object to the banishment of this forceful and self-confident Prussian. It was necessary to keep Beck as Chief of the General Staff, but the combination of Beck and Manstein was not an attractive one. A year earlier, as Commander of *Wehrkreis* I, Brauchitsch had been directed by Beck to conduct an exercise testing certain defensive measures in a specified set of conditions. He had changed the conditions and thus destroyed the point of the exercise, so Beck sent his OQuI to order him to do the whole thing all over again. The highly sensitive Brauchitsch resented the high-handedness with which Manstein performed this task, and the resentment still lingered.

Keitel's dislike for Manstein had been nursed even longer. His first important planning assignment on the Organisation Section of the General Staff had finished up in the waste paper basket when Manstein's plans for the expansion of the army were adopted. Later, with almost careless ease, this gifted officer had moved up from the Operations Section to become OQuI, Deputy Chief of the General Staff. When von Fritsch went, Beck's days were already numbered. But Keitel recognised in Manstein an even more dangerous rival, so before Beck departed his deputy had to be replaced. Thus it was with some discomfort that Keitel found himself forced to accept Manstein temporarily back in his old post. Nevertheless, he cannot fail to have been impressed by the performance of the staff work which followed, especially in contrast with the fiasco which took place in his own operations staff.

Beck and Manstein reached the Reichs Chancellery at 11 am. They conferred with Hitler for about two hours, and agreed to mobilize an army under Colonel-General von Bock, comprising VII Corps (Schobert), XIII Corps (Weichs) and 2 Panzer Division. Later, XVI Corps (Guderian) and the SS *Leibstandarte Adolf Hitler* were also added. By 6 pm Manstein had drafted the necessary mobilization concentration orders. Meanwhile, Brauchitsch had returned and, shocked at the risks of military action began a series of telephone calls appealing to Keitel to persuade Hitler to call off the operation. Keitel responded by promising to do so and 'shortly afterwards without having done it rang back to say that (Hitler) had refused'. What angered Keitel most was that General von Viebahn, Chief of the *Wehrmachtführungsamt*, his senior subordinate on the OKW, had supported Brauchitsch. Keitel's reaction caused Viebahn to suffer a nervous breakdown and lock himself in one of the rooms at the Bendlerstrasse. This was an inauspicious start for the OKW. Viebahn had been selected because he had served with distinction under General von der Schulenberg, former Chief of Staff to the Crown Prince and now an *Obergruppenführer* in the SA and SS. He was also a friend of Beck, thus he seemed to be a good choice to bridge the gulf between the OKW and the OKH.

At daybreak on 12th March the Wehrmacht crossed the Austrian frontier. Leaving Beck in Berlin, Brauchitsch and Manstein flew to Linz. They found Hitler already there, accompanied by Keitel who greeted the Army Commander-in-Chief by asking 'What on earth are you doing in Austria?' Hitler, however, accepted Brauchitsch's presence and agreed with the suggestion that he and Manstein should fly on to Vienna and supervise the absorption of the Austrian Army into the Wehrmacht. After the *Anschluss* Manstein remained in Austria for a few weeks to continue this task.

Meanwhile, Hitler had returned to Berlin, where, on 21st April, Keitel reported on the state of preparations for an invasion of Czechoslovakia. Hitler's preference was for 'a lightning-swift action as the result of

an incident (ie the assassination of the German Ambassador).' Separate thrusts penetrating the Czech fortification lines were to be 'worked out in the smallest detail (knowledge of roads, of targets, composition of columns according to their individual tasks).' Each column, Hitler stressed, must have air support: 'dive-bombers, sealing-off installations at penetration points, hampering the bringing up of reserves, destroying signals, communications traffic, thereby isolating the garrisons.' Hitler's grasp of strategy and tactics greatly impressed his listeners, especially Colonel Jodl, who had replaced Viebahn as head of the *Wehrmachtführungsamt*. When he was first appointed to the General Staff Jodl had proved himself to be a very capable staff officer. But he won the disapproval of his superiors on the OKH by his self-centred and over-ambitious attitude and so Beck unloaded him on the new OKW. He soon became one of Hitler's most devoted advisers, and far from resenting the Führer's interference in every detail of the mili-

German generals watch the invasion of Poland, *from left to right:* Manstein, Rundstedt, Keitel, Hitler, Reichenau and Rommel

tary planning, Jodl ordered one of his subordinates, Lieutenant-Colonel Zeitzler, to supply Hitler with all the minutiae of mobilization, and of the strength of the Czech fortifications and armaments.

By the end of May Jodl had the new Directive for 'Case Green' ready for Hitler's signature. It opened with the words 'It is my unalterable decision to smash Czechoslovakia by military action in the near future.' Specific instructions for the military operations included 'a thrust into the heart of Czechoslovakia ... with the strongest possible motorized and armoured units, using to the full the first success of the assault columns and the effects of the Air Force operations.' When this directive reached the OKH Brauchitsch and Beck were shocked that operational details and decisions had been made without their advice. General von Weichs noted in his diary that the idea of dismissing Jodl from the ranks of the general staff was discussed. 'It was apparent,' he wrote, 'that the command system had completely changed, but no one had been fully aware of it till then.'

Beck was particularly impressed by the Directive for 'Case Green' because on 7th May he had given Brauchitsch a memorandum which concluded that 'There are no grounds for the hope that the Czechoslovakian problem might be solved this year by military means without the intervention of Britain and France.'

Beck's assessment was based upon the reports of the German Military Attachés, especially those of General Baron Geyr von Schweppenburg and of his successor in London, Colonel Freiherr von Bechtolsheim. The Military Attachés were general staff officers selected for their tact, sociability, and military competence. According to Bechtolsheim, gentlemanly conduct was more important than a command of languages. However, the general staff was fortunate in having in Moscow at this time

The Condor Legion parades before Göring and its commanders, Richthofen, Volkmann and Sperrle

In the course of the Anschluss Hitler found in Keitel a military assistant completely subservient to his will

Ernst von Köstring, who was born and raised in Russia and who not only spoke good Russian but understood the Slav mentality. Baron von Geyr, who was in London from 1933 until 1937 was also eminently suited to his role. When first selected he was asked by Admiral Canaris to undertake the tasks of a spy. These he refused, rightly insisting that his success would be in direct proportion to the degree of 'genuine and honourable mutual understanding' he achieved. Aided by his aristocratic and cavalry background he was at first most successful and established frank and friendly relations with many senior British officers and diplomats. But after the appointment of Ribbentrop, as Ambassador, Anglo-German relations deteriorated, and in July 1937 he was obliged to take the unusual step of sending the Chief of the General Staff a report specifically contradicting that of his Ambassador. Baron Geyr's views were based upon a study of the British grand-strategic situation which he had sent to Beck in January. Whereas Germany's weakness lay in her 'inability to carry on a war of long duration owing to financial and material shortages . . . the position of the British Empire . . . is just the reverse.' The keys to British strategy were close military co-operation with France and the benevolent neutrality and economic support of the United States. 'Early (German) successes in Southern and South-Eastern Europe cannot be decisive,' Geyr warned, stressing that the British would support France in a conflict with Germany by means of economic warfare and strategic bombing. Italy and Japan will do little to reduce the strength of Britain, he predicted, because the former 'can have no real interest in a German military hegemony in Central Europe', and the latter 'is only capable of waging war for a limited time'.

In the long run Geyr was right, but he did not foresee the defeat of France (because he considered the Maginot Line was 'a barrier against a runaway German victory') or the effect it would have on the leaders of Italy and Japan. Ribbentrop, however, was prepared to base the foreign policy of Germany upon a coalition between Germany, Italy and Japan. This would tie down Britain's forces elsewhere, discourage France from fighting Germany without British support and so enable Germany to conduct a 'change of the *status quo*' in eastern Europe by force. He wrote a recommendation to this effect in January 1938 and a month later he was appointed Foreign Minister.

Nevertheless, Beck continued to base his assessment of foreign affairs on the reports of the Military Attaché Section of the General Staff. He wrote three critical memoranda during the summer of 1938. The last, on 16th July, was accompanied by an appeal to Brauchitsch to lead the collective resistance of all the generals against Hitler. But this presumed that all the generals shared the opinions of the Chief of the General Staff, which was by no means certain, as Beck himself discovered when he read a letter from Manstein, the man he had viewed as his successor. Manstein, now semi-exiled as commander of a division in Liegnitz, felt duty bound to report his thoughts to his former chief. In the first part of the letter, dated 21st July 1938, Manstein urged Beck not to resign but to continue to struggle for a reorganisation of the high command which placed the General Staff in control of the entire Wehrmacht in war, and established a closer personal relationship between the army leadership and the Führer. As far as the Czechoslovakian problem was con-cerned Manstein advised Beck to confine himself to the *military* aspects of the problem. The risk that the Western Powers might intervene, he wrote: 'is solely the responsibility of the political leadership'. (In the margin beside such statements Beck pencilled question marks.) The military leadership 'is only responsible for ensuring that a quick success is won against Czechoslovakia and that all military means are used to frighten off the French.' Manstein then went on to describe at length how an operational and tactical surprise could still be achieved in order quickly to overwhelm the Czech defences. His proposals must have seemed to Beck to bear a dishearteningly close resemblance to those of Hitler. In the draft of his reply the Chief of Staff told Manstein that though his arguments were, in the main, correct, circumstances had changed, so that 'today . . . I can only say "too late".'

Early in August Brauchitsch assembled the leading generals and read a memorandum, probably the last one Beck had given him. The reaction was pessimistic. Reichenau advised against any mass confrontation which would anger Hitler, and General Ernst Busch doubted whether it was their business to interfere in political questions. Beck replied emphatically that general staff officers had a duty to make judgements in the field of politics and grand strategy. Rundstedt, the senior serving general, urged Brauchitsch not to jeopardise his own position with Hitler. He feared that if the Commander-in-Chief was forced to resign, he would be replaced by von Reichenau. Thus the generals dispersed without coming to any decision for further action and left Beck in despair.

When Hitler heard of this meeting he ignored the senior generals and invited all the chiefs of staff of the major formations to a lunch at the Berghof on 10th August. During the afternoon Hitler spent over two hours

Alfred Jodl, the Führer's devoted adviser

explaining the reasons for his decision to settle the Czechoslovakian question. In the discussion which followed the staff officers expressed doubt that France would stand by and watch her ally invaded. Hitler countered their arguments calmly until General von Wietersheim quoted the view of his commander, General Adam, that the Western fortifications could not be held for more than three weeks. Hitler, flushed with anger, shouted that 'the West Wall could be held against any comers if only the generals were as brave as their soldiers!' After the day's events Jodl noted in his diary that 'vigour of

spirit' was lacking in the general staff officers 'because at bottom they do not believe in the genius of the Führer'. Five days later Hitler summoned the senior generals to Juterbog to hear a confirmation of his resolve to attack Czechoslovakia. Afterwards Brauchitsch refused to see Beck, and three days later the Chief of the General Staff gave up his office. On Hitler's request, 'for reasons of foreign policy,' he agreed to keep his resignation secret.

The relations between Hitler and the General Staff never recovered from the crisis of confidence caused by Beck. The murder of Schleicher and Bredow, the sordid intrigue against Fritsch and the creation of the OKW had placed heavy strains on the

Ludwig Beck, Hitler's chief critic on the General Staff

army's faith in Hitler. But Hitler's confidence in the General Staff was even more impaired by the criticisms of his policy expressed in Beck's memoranda and evidently supported not only by his contemporaries but also by the younger staff officers. After 1938 he suspected the General Staff of conspiring to thwart him at every opportunity. Far from being a valuable instrument, it had proved a great disappointment. On one occasion Hitler revealed the depth of his feelings by turning on a group of staff officers and sneering that 'Before I became Chancellor I thought that the General Staff was like a hungry dog which had to be firmly held by the collar otherwise it threatened to leap at everyone else. After I became Chancellor I had to admit that the German General Staff could not be less like a hungry dog.'

Beck's successor was General Franz Halder, who had been OQuI since Manstein's transfer. Brauchitsch had adopted the habit of circumventing Beck by working directly with Halder and found him more amenable than Beck or Manstein. Halder claimed that he accepted the appointment as Chief of the General Staff in order to continue Beck's struggle against Hitler. During the weeks leading up to the Munich crisis he was as good as his word and became involved in a plot to overthrow Hitler if he insisted on going ahead with 'Case Green'. Meanwhile, he completed the plans for the attack and, on 3rd September, von Brauchitsch took them to Hitler. Five armies were to attack Czechoslovakia: Second Army from the north-east, Eighth Army from the north, Tenth Army from the west, Twelfth Army from the south-west and Fourteenth Army from the south. But Hitler was critical; the operation was exactly what the Czechs were expecting, he complained. Second Army, facing strong defences, would become involved in 'a repetition of Verdun'.

Fourteenth Army would 'fail because of transport difficulties'. All motorized and Panzer divisions should be with Tenth Army where the defences were weakest. Their breakthrough would cut into the heart of Bohemia.

Ribbentrop leaves the embassy in London to present his credentials to the King; General Geyr, the Military Attaché, stands in the doorway behind him

Brauchitsch flustered about 'the state of the motorised divisions, supply and untrained leaders' but was cut short. Six days later Hitler called another conference. This time Brauchitsch took Halder along to explain the plan. To Hitler's astonishment Halder described the same 'pinching off' operation by Second and Fourteenth Armies which he had rejected a week before. After hearing him out, Hitler cuttingly remarked that 'We should not plan the action on the operations as we desire them, but take into consideration the probable course of action pursued by the enemy.' He then presented a well-reasoned account of the Czech defensive plans, followed by a devastating critique of the army's proposals. He was particularly disappointed at the unimaginative deployment of the Panzer and motorized formations. The motorized divisions had objectives which did not enable them to make full use of their mobility, yet Panzer divisions were to be supported by infantry on foot which would slow down their advance. 'This contradicts all the laws of logic,' Hitler told von Brauchitsch and Halder while, to add to their chagrin, Keitel stood at the Führer's elbow nodding in agreement. Again Hitler insisted on a concentration of mobile forces with Reichenau's Tenth Army.

None of this was put to the test because the Munich Conference deprived Hitler of his war in 1938. But his actions during the planning had profound effects upon the General Staff. It was now clear that the army had not only lost the struggle to control the Wehrmacht in war, it was in danger of losing control over operational and tactical matters. To make matters worse the policy of abject appeasement adopted by Britain and France seemed to discredit the gloomy predictions made by General Beck, and forced his successor into a hasty cancellation of the plans for Hitler's arrest and trial.

After the Munich Agreement the five German armies moved forward and occupied the Sudetenland and most of the fortifications they had planned to take by force. Hitler, Keitel and a small staff protected by Colonel Rommel's escort battalion deliberately avoided the OKH and accompanied the advance of Guderian's XVI Corps, part of Reichenau's Tenth Army. In March 1939 the German armies advanced again, this time under the gaze of a hostile, resentful population as they brought the ancient provinces of Bohemia and Moravia under the 'protection' of the Reich. Early in April Keitel issued two directives on 'Case White' calling for preparations for an operation against Poland 'any time from 1st September 1939 onwards'. Shortly afterwards Halder set up a 'Working Staff' comprising Colonel-General von Rundstedt, General von Manstein, Colonel Gunther Blumentritt and Major Reinhard Gehlen. Rundstedt was living at home in retirement and von Manstein was commanding a division, so most of the work fell to Blumentritt. By 7th May he had completed an 'Appreciation of the Situation'. It was obvious that by advancing from East Prussia, Silesia and Slovakia the German armies were in a favourable position to envelop the Polish forces. If the Poles had any real hope of outside help they might stand and fight west of the Vistula, but with fifty-five infantry divisions, twelve cavalry brigades and two motorized units they could only screen their frontier and keep their main concentrations in reserve. The main German thrusts from the north and south would be separated by a long thinly held sector, so Blumentritt proposed the formation of two army groups, commanded by Bock (North) and Rundstedt (South). On 26th-27th April Hitler approved the Army plan, and on 1st May the OKH sent a Concentration Directive for 'Case White' to the army group commanders. Later that month Bock and Rundstedt submitted their recommendations to OKH.

Meanwhile, the Luftwaffe and the Navy drew up their own operational plans, co-ordinated with the army plan by the inter-service liaison officers. The military and naval leaders had no

General Wietersheim

qualms about attacking Poland in order to regain Danzig and unite East Prussia again with the Reich. The grand strategic situation aroused grave concern. At the end of March Keitel met General Pariani of the Italian General Staff, but according to General Warlimont, 'Hitler expressly forbade the discussion of questions of strategy.' On 22nd May the 'Pact of Steel' was signed with Italy, but the military leaders were neither consulted nor informed about the secret protocol containing military agreements. Hitler also insisted that the plans for the attack on Poland should be kept secret from Italy and Japan. To Walter Warlimont and Bernhard von Lossberg, the senior staff officers in the *Wehrmachtführungsamt,* the Axis coalition did not seem to be sufficiently strong to discourage Britain and France from supporting Poland. But their attempt to persuade Keitel to hold a war game involving Hitler in a test of the grand strategic situation failed, and they found themselves 'in a peculiar, uneasy vacuum'.

On 23rd May Hitler held a briefing conference attended by Keitel, Warlimont, Brauchitsch, Halder, Göring, Jeschonnek, Bodenschatz, Raeder and Colonel Schmundt. After a survey of Germany's situation Hitler explained and 'Danzig is not the subject of the dispute at all. It is a question of expanding our living space to the East . . . we are left with the decision to attack Poland at the first suitable opportunity.' He hoped to isolate his victim and hinted that 'It is not impossible that Russia will show herself to be disinterested in the destruction of Poland.' But it was necessary to consider the possibility that the Western Powers might declare war. In that case, Hitler warned his military leaders, Holland and Belgium must be occupied 'with lightning speed.' If France is also defeated 'the fundamental conditions for a successful war against Britain will have been secured.' He then went on to comment on the importance of 'a wheeling movement by the Army towards the Channel ports,' and the impossibility of bringing a country to defeat by air attack alone. But the army leaders did not seem to grasp the significance of these remarks. On returning to the Bendlerstrasse they intensified preparations for the Polish campaign but made no response to Hitler's ideas of waging an offensive war in the West. Later Manstein admitted that so much had already been achieved without war that Hitler 'seemed to have an almost infallible instinct.' 'Why, we asked ourselves, should it be different this time?' At the next *Führer* Conference, on 22nd August 1939, Hitler did indeed produce another diplomatic 'bombshell' when he announced that Russia was about to sign a Non-Aggression Pact. 'I have made the political preparations,' he said. 'The way is now open for the soldier.'

The pact with Russia was seen in the General Staff as a revival of Seeckt's policy. Some of the generals, like Rundstedt, hoped that now it 'would be a *Blumenkrieg* [flower throwing war], the same as it had been in 1938 in the Sudetenland.' The majority felt that there would be fighting, but

if Russia stayed out the German army was capable of defeating Poland and achieving a stalemate leading to a negotiated peace in the West. The Chief of the General Staff certainly encouraged this view. He recorded his calculations in his diary and concluded that an early French attack

General Brauchitsch and the new Chief of the General Staff, Franz Halder, plan operations against Czechoslovakia

through the Low Countries was unlikely in view of the time required for mobilization, 'our knowledge of French operational concepts, and . . .

divisions required for the Polish campaign and for manning the 'West Wall' were to be called out 'for manoeuvres' in order not to alarm the public or escalate a crisis. The timetable required the Führer's decision regarding Y-day by 23rd August. Units in concentration areas were then to move to assembly areas for the attack. On Y-1, Hitler's order for the attack was to be given by 1200 hours. Then the mobilization of reserve divisions would take place without public proclamation, and the code word for

the political difficulties'. The French were 'more likely to react to our measures move by move'. Nevertheless, Halder began to plan the early transfer of heavy artillery from the East, the establishment of the main line of defence on the Meuse River to compensate for the lack of anti-tank guns, and the activation of more reserve divisions to build field defences along the frontier with Belgium and Holland.

The partial mobilization of reserves was due to Hitler's order that the

the timing of the assault would be sent to the service headquarters. At the same time seven divisions would man the 'West Wall', and further reserve divisions would bring Army Group 'C' (West) strength to thirty-one divisions. Everything went according to plan; the three German army groups became operational on 23rd August. Dawn on Y-day, 26th August, was set for the time of the attack. On 24th August various general staff officers moved to their wartime appointments. But at noon on 25th August Halder was surprised to receive from the OKW an enquiry about the feasibility of stopping the operation. He replied that it would not be possible after 1500 hours. At 1330 hours the OKW rescinded the order to attack. Only the very high efficiency of the General Staff's command and communication network made it possible to halt the columns moving towards the frontier. Some sabotage units could not be stopped, but the Poles assumed that the shootings which resulted were only more of the provocative frontier incidents which had occurred in recent weeks. At first there was hope that the halt meant another bloodless victory. But when Bock rang Halder to ask how far back the troops should be held he was told 'So that what should have occurred on 26th August can take place on 27th if ordered.' Halder also explained that the British had ratified their treaty with Poland and the Italians were backing away from their obligations. But after four days of uncertainty the order was given to attack at dawn on 1st September. Even then there was scepticism. Rundstedt asked the OKH when the next rescinding order might be expected and when finally 'this nonsense was to cease'. But the old general was destined never to enjoy his retirement, at 0445 hours on 1st September German troops crossed the Polish frontier.

General Blumentritt

Blitzkrieg

With the outbreak of war in 1939 the General Staff underwent a drastic change of organisation. The branches and sections required for the direction of operations became part of the HQ OKH (Headquarters Army High Command) and moved to a field command centre on the manoeuvre area at Zossen. Chief of the Army General Staff, General Halder, was in charge of this HQ. The Commander-in-Chief of the Army, Colonel-General von Brauchitsch, was also located at Zossen with a small entourage of staff officers and aides headed by Lieutenant-Colonel Curt Siewert. The *Oberquartiermeister* I, General Heinrich von Stülpnagel, was Deputy Chief of the General Staff and chief adviser to Halder in strategic and operational planning. He controlled the Operations Section and co-ordinated its work with that of other sec-

tions involved in the planning and control of operations. The OQuIV, Major-General von Tippelskirch, was responsible for the assessment of intelligence, and controlled the Foreign Armies East, Foreign Armies West and Attaché Sections. The Quartermaster General also moved to HQ OKH in order to control the supply of the Field Army and the administration of the rear areas and occupied territories. General Eugen Müller, former Commandant of the Kriegsakademie, occupied this post but he was soon forced by ill-health to hand over his duties to his Chief of Staff, Colonel Eduard Wagner. The Training, Organisation and Central Sections and the Army Transport and Army Signals Offices were placed directly under General Halder. The OQuV, General Waldemar Erfurth, remained in Berlin in charge of all the elements

Mobile anti-tank gun in the 'lightning war'

of the General Staff left there, including the Military History and the Mapping and Survey Sections, and the rear echelons of the Organisation, Training and Central Sections. The Officers' Training Section was combined with the Training Section and part of the Technical Section went into the Organisation Section. The remaining sections and the offices of OQuII and III were disbanded to free much-needed staff officers for posts on the headquarters of the armies and army groups in the field.

The role of the Chief of the General Staff was very different from that of his predecessors in the Wars of Unification and during the First World War. No longer was he chief military adviser with direct access to the head of state. Even the Commander-in-Chief of the Army lacked the influence possessed by men like von Moltke, Falkenhayn and Hindenburg, because the Führer listened more readily to the advice of Göring, Keitel and Jodl.

The leaders of the OKW were in a particularly strong position to influence Hitler because when he took to the field on 3rd September they moved with him. Nevertheless, his decision to travel around Poland in a railway train shocked the officers of the OKW. Keitel, Jodl and their aides were packed into the confined quarters along with Hitler's military and political adjutants, the service liaison officers, Party and press hangers-on, security guards, secretarial staff, and doctors. Colonel Warlimont was left in Berlin with the bulk of the OKW but with no indication of the long term strategy for the further prosecution of the war. Most of his staff had little to do but piece together information gleaned from those with the Führer and from the staffs of the three services. Each day the heads of Warlimont's Section L (National Defence) met with officers of the other offices to be briefed on the situation and to respond to the instructions or draft directives sent from the field.

General von Brauchitsch also spent much of his time visiting the headquarters of armies and corps. Thus the responsibility for the direction of operations fell upon General Halder at Zossen. Nevertheless, the Com-

Brauchitsch and his Chief Staff officer Colonel Siewert

mander-in-Chief kept in touch with the Chief of Staff and returned to Zossen when important decisions had to be taken. In contrast, Halder remained completely out of direct contact with Hitler, Keitel and Jodl. At this stage Hitler was content to leave the OKH in control of operations. Unlike those for Czechoslovakia, the plans for the Polish campaign were not the subject of major controversy. The initial German operations developed according to plan, and by 17th September the double envelopment of the Polish forces was successfully achieved when the German 'pincer movements' closed at Brest-Litovsk and the Russian army moved forward to meet its new ally. Nevertheless,

the campaign did produce a serious leadership crisis. No single, major incident was the cause, but a series of small irritations which produced in General Halder a mood of exasperation.

From various locations on his travels, Brauchitsch sent confusing and often contradictory instructions for the conduct of operations. Outside Warsaw Hitler also began to interfere in operational decisions, and to make matters worse he failed to keep his military staffs informed on political questions and diplomatic agreements. As a result when General Köstring, the Military Attaché in Moscow, telephoned Berlin to report that the Russian army would move into Poland next morning, Warlimont was completely unprepared for this information. He hastily phoned Keitel in Hitler's train. The Chief of the OKW was apparently no less surprised. He greeted the news that the Russians were advancing with the question 'Against whom?' Yet only a week earlier Halder had insisted that the OKH 'must be precisely informed concerning the political line and possible deviations. Otherwise it is impossible to act in a planned and responsible manner. The army leadership must not be exposed to political vagaries otherwise the army will lose confidence. [It is close to] the point at which confidence will break.' By the end of the campaign Halder had reached that point. In order to reassert unified leadership he urged Brauchitsch to combine the role of Commander-in-Chief with that of Chief of the General Staff while he, Halder, became First Quartermaster General.

The discussion went on into the night. Halder later described how Brauchitsch finally stated that 'he felt himself unequal to his task without my support; he needed me especially for the united struggle against Hitler . . .' He agreed to allow Halder full control of military strategy and operations, but retained the

right of final approval and signed all important directives and orders. Brauchitsch's main tasks as Commander-in-Chief were now to represent the army in Hitler's counsels and to ensure that the army was equal to its tasks by overall supervision of armaments, training, personnel, discipline and morale. This was not a satisfactory solution. But Hitler would not have accepted Halder's suggestion. The only other alternative would have been for Brauchitsch to resign. In which case the Nazi, Reichenau, would probably have become Commander-in-Chief. So Brauchitsch and Halder agreed that they should stay in office to continue the struggle against Hitler, which was already approaching a further crisis as the impatient Führer demanded a winter offensive in the West.

On 23rd May 1939 Hitler had stressed to his generals the need to strike 'with lightning speed' in the West if Britain and France entered the war. However, since the planning for Poland had begun Halder's main concern in the West had been the build up of defences. Thus it came as a shock when Warlimont leaked the news that Hitler was determined to launch a winter attack. The offensive operations in Poland had certainly been successful. But Bock had been critical of the cautiousness of the infantry and the slowness of the artillery. The Luftwaffe had too frequently bombed German troops in error. So the field commanders and the General Staff shared the opinion that much more training and greater logistical support was needed before the Wehrmacht could attack the Western Allies. When Hitler refuse to agree, the Commander-in-Chief asked his army group commanders to give him their opinions in writing. General Ritter von Leeb, an expert on defensive tactics, warned against the danger of expecting too much of the armoured and motorized forces. As in the First World War the open terrain of Poland

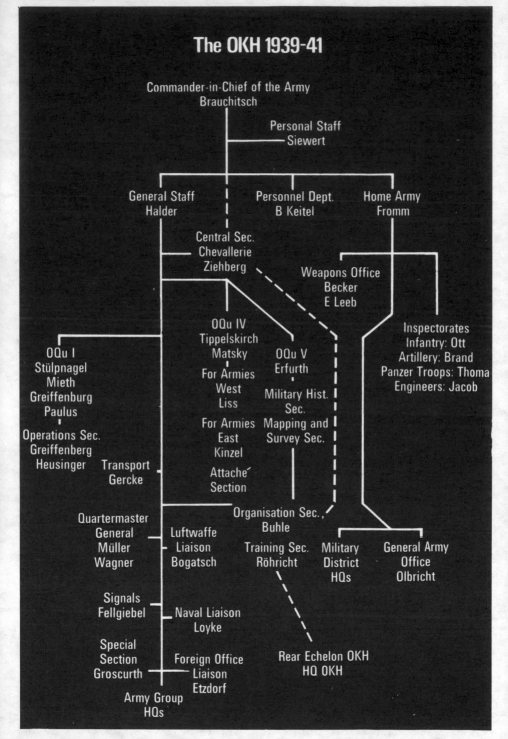

The OKH 1939-41

Commander-in-Chief of the Army
Brauchitsch

Personal Staff
Siewert

General Staff
Halder

Personnel Dept.
B Keitel

Home Army
Fromm

Central Sec.
Chevallerie
Ziehberg

Weapons Office
Becker
E Leeb

Inspectorates
Infantry: Ott
Artillery: Brand
Panzer Troops: Thoma
Engineers: Jacob

OQu IV
Tippelskirch
Matsky

OQu V
Erfurth

For Armies
West
Liss

Military Hist.
Sec.

For Armies
East
Kinzel

Mapping and
Survey Sec.

OQu I
Stülpnagel
Mieth
Greiffenburg
Paulus

Operations Sec.
Greiffenberg
Heusinger

Transport
Gercke

Attaché
Section

Quartermaster
General
Müller
Wagner

Luftwaffe
Liaison
Bogatsch

Organisation Sec.,
Buhle

Training Sec.
Röhricht

Military
District
HQs

General Army
Office
Olbricht

Signals
Fellgiebel

Naval Liaison
Loyke

Special
Section
Groscurth

Foreign Office
Liaison
Etzdorf

Rear Echelon OKH
HQ OKH

Army Group
HQs

had made mobile operations possible which were not feasible in the West. Rather than risk the political dangers of breaking Dutch and Belgian neutrality and face a repetition of the costly battles of 1915 the German army should wait for the French and British to exhaust themselves attempting to break through the 'West Wall'. General von Bock and his Chief of Staff, Salmuth, were more cautious, and consulted their army commanders. General von Kluge rejected the idea of an immediate attack. Even Reichenau, who had always been an enthusiastic exponent of motorized operations and an outspoken supporter of Hitler, responded that it would be 'criminal' to risk an offensive in the mud and fog of winter.

Halder had already heard that Göring had expressed similar concern because he could not guarantee air support in adverse weather conditions. Nevertheless, Bock hesitated to express outright opposition to Hitler. He noted in his diary: 'It was clear by mid-September that the Polish campaign was drawing to a close. Did the OKH then present the Supreme Command [Hitler] with a clear proposal for the prosecution of the war in the West or not? If not, then nobody can be surprised if the Supreme Command comes up with its own ideas – and with different ones from what the Army leaders want!' As a result, when his army commanders were summoned to Berlin, it was not Bock but Reichenau who spoke out in favour of waiting until spring. Hitler brushed such objections aside on the grounds that Germany should seize the initiative from 'the systematic French and plodding British'. But he was far from pleased with the proposal for the offensive which Brauchitsch and Halder presented. This bore a superficial similarity to the Schlieffen Plan of 1914, but it had the much more limited aim of gaining territory in the Low Countries from which to wage air and sea war against Britain. Hitler expressed his disappointment

and stated that from the start he had envisaged launching the main blow 'south of the Maas, perhaps with a subsidiary operation against Liège, in order to thrust westward and then northwestward to surround and destroy the enemy . . . advancing into Belgium.' Bock described in his diary how Brauchitsch and Halder appeared to be 'completely taken aback' by this ambitious plan. The argument which followed was so 'lively' that the conference lasted seven hours and finished with the exhausted army leaders agreeing to examine Hitler's proposal. However, Bock managed to persuade them that there was not room to concentrate and attack with sufficient force unless the whole sector from Luxembourg to Liège was used. They also reaffirmed that the right wing of the subsequent advance should be directed towards Antwerp, and accepted the danger that 'the enemy might get there first and we might bog down in a frontal attack.'

This was not acceptable, however, at the headquarters of Army Group 'A' (von Rundstedt) which had arrived to take command over the armies protecting the left flank of Bock's advance. There the Chief of Staff, Manstein, and his closest colleagues, Blumentritt and Tresckow, found it 'humiliating . . . that our generation could do nothing better than repeat an old recipe, even when this was the product of a man like Schlieffen.' Seeking a solution which would lead to more than a partial victory, Manstein found it, as Hitler had already done, in a surprise attack outflanking and enveloping the Allied forces.

The criticisms from the field commanders were not the only pressures on the Commander-in-Chief and the Chief of the General Staff. Within the OKH Lieutenant-Colonel Helmuth Groscurth was urging Brauchitsch and Halder to join a conspiracy against Hitler as the only means of resolving the crisis. The personality and influence of this gifted general staff officer are better recorded for

General Stülpnagel, Deputy Chief of the General Staff

history than those of most members of the German opposition movement because his diary and many other writings have survived. He was the son of a Bremen Protestant pastor and a mother whose family had long business associations. But he left school at the height of the First World War so it was natural that he should volunteer for the army. He distinguished himself as an ensign on the Somme, but was later twice wounded and then captured. After the war he was selected to remain in the Reichswehr but resigned because he was dismayed at the passive attitude taken by Seeckt during the events leading to the Kapp Putsch in 1920. In 1924 he rejoined and became adjutant to General von Witzleben, who later became a leading figure in the military opposition to Hitler. The understanding which developed between the two men was maintained in the years which followed while they watched with dismay as Hitler consolidated his power. In 1935 Groscurth entered the *Kriegsakademie*. His first General Staff appointment was to the *Abwehr*,

where he impressed Admiral Canaris with his directness and vigour and was soon promoted to become head of Section II, Foreign Intelligence and Counter Espionage. Under the influence of Canaris and Oster the hostility which Groscurth felt towards Hitler and his régime was intensified and directed towards decisive action. Late in 1938 the conspirators decided that they needed a man in the OKH who could exert pressure on Brauchitsch and Halder to support the opposition against Hitler. Groscurth was picked for the job, and was appointed head of the Section for Special Assignments. In addition to the small group of anti-Nazi staff officers in his section, Groscurth was supported by the Foreign Office Liaison Officer to the OKH, Hasso Etzdorf, who kept the General Staff informed of the political situation and acted as a contact between Halder and Baron von Weizsäcker, the State Secretary at the Foreign Office, who was also a strong critic of Hitler.

During the winter Groscurth circulated a number of unsigned memoranda among the senior officers of the General Staff. These were written by General Beck and passed to Groscurth by General Oster. Most of the readers were probably aware of the author's identity. But this did not deter the OQuIV, General von Tippelskirch, from pencilling critical comments in the margins, including 'Does this composition stem from an Englishman or a German? If the latter, he is overdue for a concentration camp.' But Groscurth's chief target was Halder, and during October 1939 he began to win a positive response. On the 14th the Chief of Staff told Brauchitsch that they had three choices, to attack in the West, to wait, or to bring about a 'basic transformation' by means of a revolt. While agreeing that an attack was out of the question, Brauchitsch dismissed the third choice as having the least prospect of success. It was, he said, 'negative' and would weaken Germany. They had a duty to present the military situation clearly to Hitler and 'to promote every possibility of peace'. This reply convinced Halder that he might have to proceed without Brauchitsch. So he told Groscurth to set up a planning group within the General Staff to organise a coup. It included Stülpnagel, the OQuI, Wagner, the acting QMG, Fellgiebel, the General Inspector of Signals, and Etzdorf.

But Halder was by no means decided upon a course of action. On 16th October Canaris found him in a state of 'complete nervous collapse', and von Brauchitsch 'helpless' in the conviction that if the army staged a coup the British would take advantage of the opportunity to crush Germany. Groscurth compared Halder with Moltke at the time of the Schlieffen Plan's failure and noted in his diary that 'A Chief of the General Staff has no business breaking down. Just like 1914.' When he pressed Halder on the subject of an assassination the Chief of Staff told him that for weeks he had been taking a pistol to the Reichs Chancellery but could not bring himself to use it on an unarmed man. By the end of October both Halder and Stülpnagel felt that Groscurth and Oster were pushing them too hard. But the tour of the headquarters in the West which Halder and Brauchitsch conducted early in November convinced the Chief of Staff that he

Hitler, Keitel, Jodl and the assortment of adjutants, press officers and doctors which comprised the core of the Führer HQ

Hitler plans his route with his senior adjutant, Colonel Schmundt, *right*, and the commander of his HQ, general Rommel, *left*, and General Bodenschantz, Göring's Liaison Officer with the OKW

must go ahead with a coup to avert the military disaster which would result from the attempt to conduct Operation 'Yellow', the offensive in the West, in mid-winter. He decided to give Brauchitsch a final chance to dissuade Hitler from his folly on 5th November.

The interview was a disaster. Brauchitsch repeated the familiar arguments against the attack, irritated Hitler by criticising his interference in the operations in Poland and then, worst of all, stated that the troops had shown a lack of discipline and aggressive spirit. At this Hitler shouted for Keitel, who like Halder was waiting in an ante-room. The

Chief of the OKW entered to witness a 'ghastly scene' as Hitler heaped abuse and threats upon his unfortunate Commander-in-Chief. 'The Spirit of Zossen' would be ruthlessly stamped out, he screamed, and, after forcing from Brauchitsch the admission that he could not produce specific evidence of the army's failing in Poland, he abruptly left, slamming the door behind him. Halder was horrified to see Brauchitsch emerge 'chalk-white and with a twisted countenance'. When he heard of Hitler's threats he assumed that his conspiracy was known and he arrived back at Zossen determined to destroy every shred of evidence. All thought of carrying out the coup was forgotten. Meanwhile, Hitler had issued the order for the offensive to start on 12th November. Nothing could now be done to oppose it, Halder told the shattered Groscurth. Nevertheless, in the weeks that followed Groscurth tried hard to bring

Brauchitsch and Halder back into active opposition to Hitler, especially by revealing to them the ghastly actions of the SS in Poland. But on 1st February 1940 he was informed that due to the 'lack of understanding' between himself and the Commander-in-Chief of the Army he was to be appointed a battalion commander. Though Groscurth remained on the General Staff List he regarded his removal from the OKH as 'a degradation'.

Meanwhile, bad weather and a serious breach of security had forced the postponement of Operation 'Yellow' and Halder was now beset by new pressures. After Brauchitsch's humiliating failure on 5th November, it was clear to most of the military leaders that all efforts would now have to be concentrated upon the successful conduct of the offensive. 'The Army has been given its task, and it will fulfil that task!' von Rundstedt told his subordinate commanders on 11th November in an effort to counter the pessimistic impression made by Brauchitsch and Halder during their visit a week before. The old general had already endorsed the alternative plan produced by his Chief of Staff, but Manstein's ideas won very little response from the OKH. Their resemblance to Hitler's proposals was enough to condemn them, and in any case both Brauchitsch and Halder regarded von Manstein as 'too clever by half'. Rundstedt was bluntly told that the mobile forces required for such an operation were not available. However, Hitler, who no longer saw any necessity to respect the advice of the OKH, independently ordered the transfer of Guderian's XIX Panzer Corps to Army Group 'A' to be used against the area around Sedan.

At first Guderian was displeased at the resulting dispersion of the Panzer forces, but when he saw Manstein's plan he responded with 'unbounded enthusiasm.' Hitler's next move was to issue a directive stating that 'All arrangements are to be made in order

Admiral Canaris, Chief of Counter-Espionage

to shift the main effort quickly from Army Group 'B' to Army Group 'A' in case faster and greater success can be achieved at 'A' . . . as one might well anticipate from the present distribution of enemy forces.' Though this indicated that Hitler was sympathetic to their ideas, von Rundstedt and Manstein still had difficulty in convincing Brauchitsch and Halder. By January they had written six major memoranda and numerous letters on the subject, but Halder and Stülpnagel merely replied that though they agreed with the Army Group's ideas, the final decision lay in Hitler's hands. The memoranda were passed neither to the Operations Section nor to Hitler. An attempt by Rundstedt and Manstein to have their memorandum of 12th January submitted to Hitler was rejected by Brauchitsch. A month later von Manstein was 'promoted' to command an infantry corps and replaced by Sodenstern. In this way the OKH got rid of another 'importunate nuisance' who, like Groscurth, had become an embarrassment to his superiors. Nevertheless, worn down by Manstein's submissions, Halder agreed to attend the army group war game on 7th February at which Manstein's plan was tested. At this and a second war game a week later Halder began to recognise the advantages of the Army Group 'A' plan. So, too, did Hitler who had re-

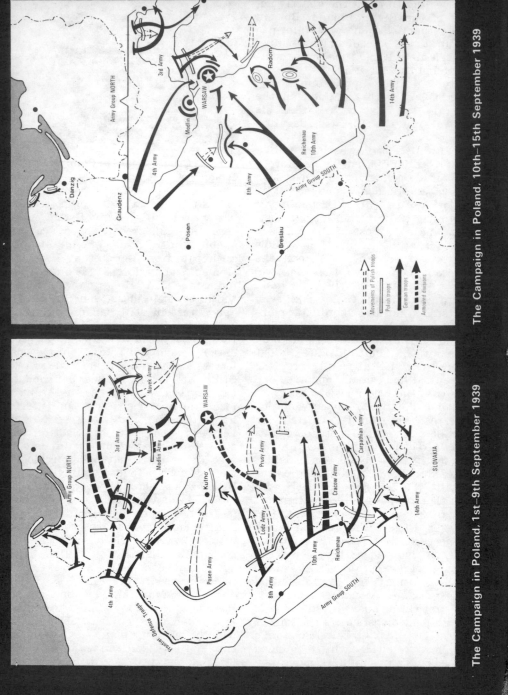

The Campaign in Poland. 10th–15th September 1939

The Campaign in Poland. 1st–9th September 1939

Croningen

Amsterdam

Rotterdam

Fortress Holland

Grebbe Line

Ijssel Position

Army Group C.

7th Army

Antwerp

Koln

Rhein

BEF

Liege

Army Group A.

Namur

Koblenz

Maubeuge

1st Army

Mainz

9th Army

2nd Army

Verdun

3rd Army

Army Group B.

Metz

4th Army

5th Army

Tuul

Maginot Line

8th Army

Maginot Line

Belfort

Concentration for Operation 'Yellow', 10th May 1940

General Falkenhorst, who commanded the invasion of Norway and Denmark

quested details of the army's proposed dispositions down to battalions, batteries and tanks. He expressed doubt about the concentrations of armour opposite the fortified areas around Liège and again suggested that they would be better used at Sedan. The Chief of the Operations Section, Colonel von Greiffenberg, and his senior assistant, Lieutenant-Colonel Adolf Heusinger, were ordered to study Hitler's ideas. A few days later Hitler had dinner with the new corps commanders. Among them was Manstein, who seized the opportunity to present his plan for the offensive in the West. Meanwhile, Halder had modified his ideas and the following day, 18th February, he presented Hitler with a drastically modified plan and an analysis of the best disposition of the armoured forces for a spring offensive. Bock's Army Group 'B' was reduced to two armies (18th and 6th), while Rundstedt now had the 4th, 12th, 16th and 2nd Armies with three-quarters of the mobile forces. After a long period of dissension, despair, uncertainty and obtuseness the General Staff suddenly began to work with enthusiasm and efficiency. When von Rundstedt and his staff, deprived of Manstein's clear vision, began to doubt the validity of pushing the tanks to the forefront, Halder replied curtly that the time for First World War methods was past.

Hardly had the disagreement over the offensive in the West been resolved than a new problem confronted Halder. On 21st February Colonel Heusinger reported to him that Hitler had summoned General von Falkenhorst and put him in charge of the invasion of Norway and Denmark. His XXI Corps Headquarters was to be placed directly under the OKW and given command over the 7th Parachute Division, three infantry divisions, a mountain regiment and a motorized rifle brigade. Halder was incensed, and noted in his diary, 'Not a word had been exchanged on this subject between the Führer and the C-in-C (Brauchitsch).' When Falkenhorst and his Chief of Staff, Colonel Buschenhagen, visited Halder a few days later they got a cold reception. The Chief of Staff demanded a promise that he would be consulted again before the OKW made a formal request for troops. Nevertheless, Fal-

kenhorst later reported to Hitler that two complete mountain divisions would be required, and the OKW went ahead and drew up a directive and a list of the formations required for 'Case Weser Exercise' without the further involvement of the General Staff. Halder's concern was not merely that significant forces were being divered from Operation 'Yellow'; he was also deeply perturbed at the change in command procedure which had placed the OKW in direct control of the Norwegian operation and left the General Staff of the Army entirely out of the planning. Göring was also furious that Luftwaffe formations were directly subordinated to Falkenhorst. He succeeded in persuading Hitler that requests for air support should be directed via the OKL. Thus the Führer conference on 'Weser Exercise' on 5th March was dominated by the voluble and critical Göring, while Brauchitsch demonstrated his displeasure with cold formality.

The conduct of 'Weser Exercise' by the OKW went fairly smoothly, but there were some moments of crisis, especially when the German naval

German vessels sunk by the Royal Navy in Narvik fjord

Tank crews receive briefing before the
assault; France, 1940

forces in Narvik fjord were destroyed
by the Royal Navy, leaving Major-
General Dietl and his mountain troops
cut off. Hitler decided that Narvik
would have to be abandoned and that
Dietl should try to march to Trond-
heim, but Jodl persuaded him that it
would be better to let him hold out in
the mountains and send relief by land.
Colonel Schmundt, Hitler's adjutant,
and Lieutenant-Colonels Boehme and
von Lossberg of the *Wehrmachtführungsamt* were sent to Norway to
assess the situation there. These competent general staff officers quickly
recognised that the British troops in
northern Norway were in an even
more precarious situation than the
Germans. In spite of the heavy losses
suffered by the German Navy, the
British had difficulty in supporting
their troops by sea because the Luftwaffe dominated the air. Its operations were skilfully controlled by 5th
Air Fleet Headquarters established in

Oslo by General Erhard Milch, the
Luftwaffe's most senior administra-
tor. In May Milch handed over the
General Stumpff and returned to the
West where Operation 'Yellow' was
about to begin.
    The reputation of the German
General Staff in the Second World
War rests chiefly upon its conduct of
the *Blitzkrieg* through the Low Countries and France in 1940. In Poland the
enemy had fought doggedly but was
ill-equipped and in a hopeless strategic position from the start. In
attacking Russia the General Staff
committed the greatest blunder in its
history by challenging a vast state organised for total war with a Wehrmacht based on a limited war economy. But in France the material
factors were fairly even. It was a
campaign in which the achievement
of a decisive victory depended upon
superior leadership, strategy and
tactics.
    Once the period of doubt and conflict
over *whether* to attack in the West
had passed General Halder was able to

concentrate his mind upon the question *how* to attack. Finally acknowledging the merit of the Army Group 'A' plan for the breakthrough, he remained uncertain of what the objective of the Panzer thrust should be. However, he recognised that Rundstedt would need more than three armies as suggested by Manstein. He decided that the main thrust from the Ardennes would be conducted by List's Twelfth Army, with Kluge's Fourth and Busch's Sixteenth Armies on its flanks. As the Twelfth Army advanced it would need further flank support in order to maintain contact with the Fourth Army. So Halder added the Second Army (Weichs) to Rundstedt's army group. Furthermore, seven of the ten Panzer divisions were allocated to Army Group 'A'. This left Bock's Army Group 'B' with only two armies, Küchler's Eighteenth and Reichenau's Sixth. Bock, convinced that this was a mistake, visited Halder and pleaded with him to shift the weight of the attack back to Army Group 'B'. He accused the Chief of the General Staff of 'gambling with Germany's fate'. By adopting the 'adventurous plan' of striking through the forested Ardennes Mountains he would become 'the grave-digger of the Panzer arm'. Halder calmly replied that it was precisely this unusual deployment that would achieve surprise. The previous plan, he admitted, would merely have pushed the enemy back. Nevertheless, the interview left Halder anxious about Bock's conduct of the campaign. Normally a temperamental *prima donna* of a commander like Bock would have been given a Chief of Staff whose steadiness and loyalty to the General Staff and its Chief was not in doubt. Unfortunately the man most suited for the post, Sodenstern, had already been transferred from Army Group 'C' to 'A' in place of the over-confident Manstein. Bock's Chief of Staff, General Hans von Salmuth was as 'difficult' as Manstein but lacked his aristocratic poise and was,

Lieutenant Witzig, the leader of the paratroops who captured the fortress of Eben Emael

in Halder's estimation, disagreeable and impatient. But such was the shortage of senior general staff officers that Halder had no choice but to leave Salmuth with Bock.

In fact the success of the campaign dispelled Bock's fears. In Holland General Student's paratroops seized key bridges and airfields, and the ground assult, spearheaded by 9th Panzer Division, rushed to link up with them. In Belgium glider-borne troops and parachutists seized two bridges over the Albert Canal and landed on the roof of the fortress of

Eben Emael. Using flame throwers and the hollow-charge explosives developed under Hitler's personal direction, they paralysed the fort until a force of assault engineers led by Colonel Mikosch arrived to complete the work and open up the Belgian defences to the main thrust of General Hoepner's XVI Panzer Corps. The British and French assuming this to be the main German blow rushed headlong into Belgium.

For Halder, sitting in the OKH Field Headquarters, there was little to do but to note the successes and failures of the initial assault and the reports of the progress of Kleist's great armoured columns moving through Luxembourg. By the third day of the offensive the Chief of the General Staff was confident that Bock could pin down the enemy armies in Belgium while Rundstedt's thrust cut across their rear. By 17th May he felt able to shift Bock's only Panzer corps south to support those of Kleist and Hoth which were already half way to the Channel.

Kleist could hardly believe the ease with which his Panzer forces crossed the Meuse at Sedan and he ordered them to wait in the bridgehead for more infantry support. Guderian phoned Kleist and his Chief of Staff, Colonel Kurt Zeitzler, and tactlessly reminded them of the similar hesitations which had marred the execution of Schlieffen Plan in 1914. But as the Panzer corps broke out into the plain of Flanders, Halder still had doubts about the further development of the operation, and favoured a swing to the south-west, taking in Paris with the right wing, and turning south-east to attack the Maginot Line from the rear. This brought him into conflict with Hitler who wanted to push on northwestwards to the coast, but was anxious not to over extend the Panzer forces before List's infantry had formed a defensive line on the south flank. Generals von Rundstedt and von Kleist felt the same concern and this resulted in another halt of the

Panzer corps and angry recriminations from Guderian. Nevertheless, his tanks reached Abbeville on 20th May before anyone had decided where they should go from there. Halder again argued that the main thrusts should turn south-east, and seemed content to leave the final destruction of the trapped Belgian, French and British armies to Army Group 'B'. But Brauchitsch, over-estimating the strength of a British counterattack at Arras, was convinced that a 'great battle' was developing.

The uncertainty at the OKH about the situation at the head of the Panzer wedge was partly caused by the behaviour of the commanders of the Panzer divisions and corps, who were frequently in the thick of the battle and out of contact with their own staffs. For example, Erwin Rommel, then commanding 7th Panzer Division, arrived in Dinant on 13th May, but could not get his command and signals vehicle down to the River Meuse where the assault crossing was taking place. So he went ahead on foot with an adjutant and became pinned down by enemy fire from the opposite bank. He then commandeered a Mark IV tank and drove down the valley. Again he came under fire and his adjutant was wounded in the arm. Returning to his divisional headquarters he found his superiors, General von Kluge and General Hoth there. But he was soon off again on foot and 'took over personal command of the 2nd Battalion of 7th Rifle Regiment and for some time directed operations'. The following day, while he was accompanying his Panzer Regiment's attack, the Panzer III in which he was travelling was hit twice and he was wounded in the face and forced to abandon the stricken tank. Recording these events later he attributed his success in holding and expanding the bridgehead to 'the fact that the divisional commander with his signals troop kept on the move and was able to give his orders direct to the regiment commanders in the forward line. Wireless alone – due to the necessity for encoding – would have taken far too long, first to get the situation reports back to Division and then for Division to issue its orders. Continuous wireless contact was maintained with the division's operations staff, which remained in the rear, and a detailed exchange of views took place early each morning and each afternoon between the commander and his Ia (Operations Officer). This method of command proved extremely effective.' Even the Panzer corps commanders got involved in battalion engagements. Guderian was 'anxious to take part in the assault across the Meuse by the riflemen' and 'went over in the first assault boat'. The Rifle Regiment commander greeted him with the comment that 'Joy riding in canoes on the Meuse is forbidden!' But this was not the only reason why Guderian's superiors lost radio contact with him. After the attempts to restrain his advance he set up an advanced headquarters and laid miles of field telephone wire linking it with his corps headquarters so that he did not need to communicate with his own staff by radio which could be monitored by the OKH or OKW.

Commanders like Guderian and Rommel placed a heavy responsibility on their general staff officers. Back at corps or division headquarters the Ia was often obliged to make important decisions on behalf of his absent commander, but above all he had to maintain the 'rhythm and routine' of collecting and assessing information, drafting and issuing orders, and reporting the situation to the higher headquarters. Everything had to be geared to the issuing of orders for the next day. Corps headquarters usually issued its orders as early in the evening as possible in order to give the divisional staffs time to draw up their orders and get them to regiments.

The staff officer Ic provided information about the enemy, Ib contributed the details of supply, transport and administration, the rest was the responsibility of the Ia, who issued the final order. Most of its contents were compiled during the course of the day as each of the contributors completed his share and discussed its implications with the Ia. The most important elements, the formation's intention, organisation and tasks for the next day depended upon the orders from the next higher formation. The Ia and his assistant (*Ordonnanzoffizier*) and Ia's clerk would then prepare a draft order for approval or amendment by the commanding general on his evening return from visits to the front. This done, the headquarters went into action typing, duplicating, signalling, telephoning, dispatching through the night. Early next morning the Ic began the staff's work again by collecting information from the front and from other formations. This was assessed and sent to the next higher headquarters in the early forenoon. Meanwhile, the Ib was also collecting information on the supply situation on which to base his requests for replenishment. At noon the commanding general would either return to the headquarters or contact the Ia by field telephone or radio in order to exchange information and discuss the situation in order to reach agreement on the broad intent of the orders for the next day.

This routine had to be flexible for it was often broken as a result of enemy action. But it could also be damaged by the decision of a higher headquarters to do something unpredictable or unexpected in the light of current situation reports and the overall intention of the operations. This is why the decisions to change the pace or direction of the Panzer thrust across Flanders aroused such dismay and anger in the field commanders and their staffs. Orders already drafted had to be scrapped, and those issued had to be countermanded, bringing a danger of confusion, frustration and error on the battlefield. In 1940 the fault for this lay partly with Halder who until the third week of May envisaged a great curving sweep, touching Paris and turning to take the French army in the rear. On the other hand he did not agree with Brauchitsch's decision on 23rd May to put Army Group 'B' in control of the last phase of the envelopment battle in Flanders, which, he noted, 'would get us into considerable difficulties owing to the personalities of the commander (Bock) . . . and his staff (Salmuth).' Next day during a visit to Rundstedt's headquarters, Hitler heard about this decision and promptly cancelled it. But with Rundstedt's agreement he also halted the Panzer Groups of Kleist and Hoth. The reason given for this inconsistency was that, instead of the two army groups, the Luftwaffe would finish off the encircled enemy. Guderian and his staff were 'utterly speechless' when they received the halt order. Halder was also angry. Having apparently shelved the idea of turning south-east he now wanted 'to make Army Group"A" the hammer and Army Group "B" the anvil' for the destruction of the British Expeditionary Force. But by the time the halt order was finally cancelled the Panzer Groups were recuperating from their past exertions and making preparations for the attack across the Somme. The impetus of the offensive had been lost. The British had stiffened their defences and organised the evacuation by sea. 'We must look on while countless thousands of the enemy sail off to England under our noses,' complained Halder bitterly.

While the strategic direction of the campaign suffered from conflict and uncertainty at the top, the operational and administrative skill of the controlling staffs was undeniable. As soon as Kleist had won his bridgehead across the Meuse, a massive movement began which drew formations from all three army groups, the OKH reserve and the Home Army. Troops on foot, horse-drawn and motor trans-

port columns, and troop trains all converged upon the narrow corridor from Sedan to the sea. The co-ordination and control of the road and rail movement of men, equipment and supplies must stand as one of the greatest achievements of the German General Staff in the Second World War. As a result the Germans were able to launch the second phase of the campaign in the West (Operation 'Red') on the 5th June, by storming across the Aisne and the Somme. Nevertheless, the campaign plan was agreed upon only after the usual differences of opinion between Hitler and the Chief of the General Staff. In the initial proposal Halder departed from his earlier concept and placed the armour on the right wing to pass *west* of Paris. Hitler, however, insisted that Halder should amend the plan so that the main thrust should pass *east* of Paris and threaten the rear of the Maginot Line. On 29th May Brauchitsch and Halder met with the army group and army commanders at Charleville for a final briefing conference. With 120 divisions in the line and twenty-three more in the OKH reserve against only sixty-five French divisions there was little doubt about the outcome. The only discordant note was expressed by Küchler who was having difficulty in breaking through the British rear-guards at Dunkirk. The idea of pursuing the defeated enemy across the Channel was not even discussed. Three weeks later, with France conquered, the General Staff still had no plans for the continuation of the war. The defeat of France was not the only event which changed the strategic balance in Europe in June 1940. Italy also entered the war, and Russia moved closer to the Rumanian oil fields by annexing Bessarabia. But the German leaders were confident that the war was nearly over. Hitler went off on a sight-seeing tour in France. The OKW Section 'L' was left for a while in the Black Forest. Jodl worked on a memorandum on the prosecution of the war against Britain which was based on the conviction that 'the final German victory over England is only a matter of time'. Meanwhile the OKH prepared to move to Fontainebleau, and Halder began optimistically planning the establishment of the 'peace-time Army'.

Not all the generals were quite so complacent. Colonel von Lossberg of Section 'L', visiting Manstein, found him disappointed that no pursuit of the British had been improvised when they were getting out of France. The defeat of the rest of the French army was far less important. The Naval leaders, who gave more thought to grand strategy than the generals, had always considered Britain as the main enemy. On 21st May, Admiral Raeder suggested that a cross-channel invasion might be necessary, but air and naval blockade still seemed to be the best means of achieving victory. On 17th June Warlimont told the Chief of Naval Operations that the OKW had not carried out any preparatory work for a landing. Admiral Fricke had been working on the problem but he had no grounds for optimism. The losses off Norway ruled out any fleet action. However, he hoped that light naval forces could land troops on the English coast. But the OKH had not yet given serious consideration to this possibility. On 21st June the naval liaison officer at the OKH reported that 'the General

Staff is not concerning itself with the question of England: considers execution impossible'. This inactivity aroused concern at Army Group 'B' Headquarters and General von Salmuth criticised Halder for not regrouping the forces in France on the Channel coast in preparation for a crossing. Halder noted that Salmuth was 'obviously the trouble-maker in Army Group 'B'. He has once again told his Commander that our regrouping plans are an insult to him (Bock) and that he might as well go on leave and let the army group veterinary take over his duties.' Bock thoroughly agreed with his Chief of Staff and remarked sarcastically that all he had to do on the Bay of Biscay was 'to watch out that the sea-shore wasn't carried away or the demarcation line stolen.'

A few days later General Halder suddenly became aware that the war against Britain must be brought to a swift end. While visiting Berlin he learned from Baron von Weizsäcker at the Foreign Office that Hitler's eyes were already turned eastward, and that he considered that England would need only another 'demonstration of our military power before she gave up and left our rear free for the East.' So on returning to Fon-

General Rommel, commander of 7th Panzer Division, during a lull in the battle

tainebleau the Chief of the General
Staff summoned Colonel von Greiffenberg, Head of the Operations Section and told him that planning must
commence immediately for military
action against England and Russia.

These tasks placed a heavy burden on
the General Staff. The OQuI, Stülpnagel was in charge of the Armistice
Commission, so Greiffenberg was ordered to take over his duties, and
reorganise the Operations Section

Guderian in his armoured command vehicle

into working groups so that it could handle both problems in the coming weeks. As a further assistance to Greiffenberg, Halder called Major-General Erich Marcks, the Chief of Staff of Küchler's Eighteenth Army which was about to take command in the East, and Lieutenant-Colonel Feyerabend, Ia of XXXX Corps, to carry out independent studies for an invasion of Russia.

The shortage of general staff officers at the top was symptomatic of the situation throughout the army. On 1st September there were 824 general staff positions and only 811 trained and partly trained staff officers to fill them. This left no replacements for losses and, with the closing of the *Kriegsakademie*, no means of training new men. The hope that the conflict would be localized and short was shattered on 3rd September when Britain and France declared war. By the end of the Polish campaign the establishment of further formations had created a need for twenty more staff officers. Former staff officers commanding field units and officers who had failed the *Kriegsakademie* course had to be placed in general staff appointments. At the same time the Central Section of the General Staff under Colonel von der Chevallerie studied the general staff training conducted in the First World War, when trainees were sent to formation headquarters to learn by experience. The study concluded that the positional warfare in the West would not meet the needs of training and recommended a series of eight-week courses instead. On 18th November Halder ordered each corps command to nominate at least three officers for the course commencing on 1st January 1940 at Dresden. Colonel von Witzleben was appointed Commander, with a deputy, and four instructors. The curriculum contained a condensed version of the most important sub-jects taught at the *Kriegsakademie*. Of the sixty trainees, forty-four passed and were allocated as follows: OKW and OKH – 11, Army group staffs – 4, army staffs – 5, divisional staffs – 13, reserve – 7, other – 4. The second course from 7th April – 14th June 1940 comprised forty-six trainees of which all but three went to the general staff. Although only five staff officers were killed in the campaign in the West, the demand still exceeded the supply. In June it was 1,005 posts and in the autumn it reached 1,117 as the Wehrmacht continued to grow to meet the demands of Hitler's strategy.

In spite of the obvious difficulties the army leaders began their planning for the invasion of England in a mood of cheerful optimism. A State Secretary in the Ministry of Economics suggested the construction of amphibious 'war crocodiles' of ferro-concrete which would carry tanks and artillery across the Channel and climb the beach on caterpillar tracks. Major-General von Schell, Head of the Mechanized Transport Group in the OKH, was experimenting with troop carrying boats powered with aircraft engines and capable of 50 mph. More realistically, General Emil Leeb, Chief of the Army Weapons Office, reported to Halder that 100 Mark III and twenty Mark IV tanks had been made submersible, ferries were being adapted to carry up to forty tanks, and new smoke bombs were being developed. Admiral Schniewind, Chief of the Naval Staff, assured Halder that he was fairly confident provided that there was calm weather for the crossing and that the Luftwaffe won air superiority, 'in which case the landing might not even be necessary'. Lieutenant-Colonel Liss, Head of the Foreign Armies West Section, estimated that the British had only fifteen to twenty divisions of fighting value. But Keitel regarded this intelligence as 'meagre and not very reliable' and described a landing as 'extremely difficult'. Admiral Raeder was more cautious than his subordinates on the

The Führer arrives for the surrender
ceremony at the historic railway
carriage in the Compiègne forest

Naval Staff and told Hitler that a
landing should be regarded as 'a last
resort'. He also warned Brauchitsch
on 17th July that the risk was great
enough to involve the loss of the
entire invasion force, but the army
chief did not seem impressed. Hitler,
however, was well aware of the dangers. He told his military chiefs on
21st July that it would be an 'excep-
tionally daring undertaking', '. . . not
just a river crossing, but the crossing
of a sea . . . dominated by the enemy'.
Nevertheless, the OKH continued to
insist upon a broad crossing by the
three armies (16th, 9th and 6th) side
by side. Raeder, therefore, sent the
General Staff a memorandum which,
Halder complained, 'upset all previous
calculations'. Greiffenberg was sent
off to Berlin and returned to confirm
that the navy might not be able to
undertake 'Operation Sea Lion' in

1940. Brauchitsch and Halder began
to discuss a campaign in the Mediterranean, including an attack on Gibraltar, Panzer support for the Italians
in North Africa, an offensive from
French Syria on Palestine, and a
campaign to take the Suez Canal. In
order to strain British military resources Russia might be invited to
drive towards the Persian Gulf. Only
nine days earlier an autumn attack
on Russia had been discussed with
Hitler, but rather than become involved in a two-front war the army
leaders now preferred to remain
friendly with Stalin until Britain had
been defeated. Next day, 31st July,
Hitler revealed that he understood
the Navy's difficulties, and was prepared to consider side-shows in the
Mediterranean, but first he would
unleash the Luftwaffe on England and
if the results were unsatisfactory then
preparations for a crossing would be
halted. If, however, the British seemed
'shattered' then the landing would
take place. In any event Britain's

position would become hopeless in 1941 because in May he intended to strike down the Soviet Union. Russia's defeat would make Japan an even greater threat to the USA and thus prevent her from supporting Britain. To meet the needs of this grand strategy an army of 180 divisions would be needed, 120 against Russia and sixty to hold western Europe. Furthermore, the German domination would have to be extended over Rumania to ensure the security of the oilfields there. These decisions determined the direction of German strategy for the next year. The war economy was dominated by the need to provide the massive army with equipment, including a doubling of the Panzer and motorized divisions. German relations with Finland, Hungary, and Rumania were also immediately affected.

General Salmuth, who criticised Halder for not regrouping the forces in France in preparation for a Channel crossing

After the conference Halder flew back to Fontainebleau where he found that Major-General Marcks had completed his study for an invasion of Russia. He expressed general agreement and told Marcks to start work on the organisation and transportation problems. Meanwhile the Chief of the General Staff turned back to 'Sea Lion', and spent much of his time in August in a drawn-out squabble with the navy on the question of the breadth of the landing front. The navy could only support a narrow landing between Folkestone and Eastbourne, but Halder rejected this as complete suicide. 'I might as well put the troops . . . straight through a sausage machine.' He was also bitter about the Luftwaffe's slow start in mounting the bombing offensive, and complained that the OKW, now that it was really confronted with a tri-service operation, 'played possum'. By the end of September the Luftwaffe's failure to win air superiority made him anxious to see 'Sea Lion' shelved till the following spring. But he was also irritated by Hitler's requests for studies of operations in the Mediterranean, the Iberian peninsula, and the Balkans and expressed the fear that if Germany became too deeply involved in the south-east it might result in a postponement of the attack on Russia.

Hitler seems to have been well aware of Halder's critical attitude and he excluded the army and navy staffs from participation in his abortive effort to establish a grand strategic coalition against Britain in the Mediterranean. To bring the rivals, Italy, Spain and Vichy France into an alliance was an ambitious undertaking even for Adolf Hitler. But, breaking with his usual habit of summoning foreign statesmen to his presence, he set off in October to visit Mussolini, Laval, Pétain and Franco. The talks were inconclusive, but Mussolini dealt the idea of a coalition a final blow when he changed his mind about co-operating with Vichy France and demonstrated his desire to assert his independence by invading Greece. The military fiasco which resulted forced Hitler to plan a military campaign to push the British out of Greece next spring (Operation 'Marita'). But he was not able to do the same at Gibraltar because he made the mistake of sending Canaris to exert pressure on General Franco to co-operate and the Admiral,

Above: Colonel Greiffenberg,
Head of the Operations Section.
Right: Paris, 1940

anxious to prevent a further extension of the war, did just the opposite. The hopes of a Russian offensive towards the Persian Gulf which Ribbentrop and Jodl fostered in Hitler were also dashed. Molotov arrived in Berlin in November and showed that he and his cynical master in the Kremlin were much more concerned about Germany's massive 'Military Mission' in Rumania and secret negotiations with Finland than with speculative expeditions to carve up the empire of the British, whose bombers were active enough to force the diplomats into an air raid shelter in the middle of the conversations. Even the idea of supporting the Italians in North Africa was tempor-

General Franco visits Berlin in October 1940

arily abandoned when Thoma, the Inspector General of Mobile Troops, returned from a visit there and described to Hitler the Italians' lack of readiness for offensive operations and the difficulties of supply without adequate bases or control of the sea routes.

The confusion and uncertainty in the OKH was reflected in General Halder's address to the Chiefs of Staff

of the army groups and armies who assembled at Zossen on 13th December. He laid stress on Britain and stated that although Operation 'Sea Lion' was postponed, preparations would continue so that it could be undertaken at a favourable moment. Similarly Operation 'Felix' against Gibraltar might also be revived. Operation 'Marita', however, would proceed to ensure that the British held no air or naval bases in Greece. It was Germany's policy to exploit France, but should she show 'definite signs of illoyalty (sic)' the rest of France would be seized (Operation 'Attila'). Halder lamented the loss of Axis prestige caused by Italy's defeats. Russia posed no immediate threat but would try to exploit any Axis weakness. Thus 'the decision over the hegemony in Europe will be achieved in a struggle with Russia. Therefore, preparations will be made to move against Russia if the political situation permits.'

Halder stated that these vast operations would strain the organisation of the army, and warned that staff officers should not complain but co-operate and maintain standards. Nevertheless, the expansion of the army would necessitate 180 new general staff appointments, thus there would be some 'watering down' in the formation headquarters below army level. Army chiefs of staff would have to exert a personal influence on the training and education of new staff officers. He then went on to warn his colleagues not to expect honour or recognition for their efforts, but to remember the motto 'Achieve much, appear little.' At the end of the day's conference he noted in his diary; 'The need to be constantly ready to fulfil political demands causes discomforts and frictions . . . We will overcome them and fulfil every task which is set us.' At this time the confidence inspired by the victory over France still dominated his attitude. Within a year all this was shattered by the failure of Operation 'Barbarossa'.

The planning for Operation 'Barbarossa' was not the work of the Chief of the General Staff alone, but was delegated by General Halder to various subordinates. When Major-General Marcks, Colonel Feyerabend and Colonel Kinzel had completed their preliminary studies, these were handed over to General Friederich Paulus, who became OQuI on 3rd September 1940. Paulus was a very shy and reticent personality, but, like Jodl, he was an enthusiastic supporter of Hitler. Before the war he had been Guderian's chief of staff and had developed his ideas about the use of armoured forces. But he was also very methodical and precise in the exercise of his duties and was therefore selected to be Chief of Staff to the volatile Reichenau in Poland and the West. His appointment as OQu I was a tactful replacement of the conservative Stülpnagel by an officer who would give the General Staff a more 'modern' look in Hitler's eyes.

In November Paulus began a series of war games to test plan 'Otto' which he had developed from the Marcks study. He also ordered the chiefs of staff of the three army groups in the East to carry out independent operation studies. The work of Generals Brennecke, Salmuth and von Sodenstern confirmed the conclusion reached by Paulus that Moscow must be the main objective. But Sodenstern doubted that the capture of the city would be decisive. He suggested that Leningrad, Moscow and Kharkhov should be taken as bargaining counters for a peace giving Germany domination over the Baltic seaboard and the Ukraine. The other generals tended to assume that the capture of Moscow would have to be decisive because other significant objectives such as the Caucasian oilfields or the industrial centre east of the Volga lay beyond the range of the single campaign which Hitler demanded. Paulus himself was perturbed by the difficulty of relating the forces available to the space to be covered and the time available between May and October in which to achieve victory. But he was not the man to formulate such doubt into a significant argument. General Mueller Hillebrand, then adjutant to Halder, illustrated his hesitancy by describing how a high spirited junior staff officer returning from a Christmas party had rung the neck of a pet goose which Paulus kept behind his quarters. Instead of having the matter out next morning, the OQu I brooded about it for several days and refused to eat at the mess table until his adjutant persuaded the offender to submit a formal apology. Later, at Stalingrad, Paulus's hesitation to act sealed the fate of his Sixth Army. But his failure to express his doubts about the plan for the invasion of Russia in 1940 had even worse consequences for the German Army as a whole. While Paulus remained silent Halder presented the plan to Hitler on 5th December.

Halder himself did not have a very critical eye for strategic matters. His so-called war diary or daily notebook shows that he was in fact overwhelmed by the petty detail of military administration. According to Mueller Hillebrand, he rose at five and went horse riding until seven-thirty. After breakfast he received the morning reports from the field army, then heard the views of his section heads and discussed the current situation. He then received liaison officers until about eleven o'clock. For the next hour he conferred with various subordinates on a great multiplicity of administrative matters until noon when they went to lunch. He did not eat lunch but used the next hour to read through the mass of papers which accumulated on his desk. Then the flow of visitors began again until dinner between 8 and 9 p m , after which the Chief of Staff refreshed himself for the next round of work by taking a short sleep. He then worked on his correspondence and his notebook into the night until 2.30 am or later. It should be remembered that Halder came from a family with a 300-year tradition of service in the Bavarian Army. The Bavarian general staff tended to be drawn from the bureaucratic middle-class rather than from the aristocracy. It is difficult to imagine Prussians like Rundstedt, Bock or Manstein tieing themselves to a routine like Halder's and delegating as important a matter as the operations plan against Russia to their

Brauchitsch and Halder at a Führer conference on 'Barbarossa'

subordinates.

After the war Halder and others asserted that his delegation of the planning was due to his 'inner rejection' of the idea of aggression against Russia. He is also described as opposing Hitler's decision to attack and warning him of the strength of the Soviet Union. The contemporary documents, including the general's own notebooks, do not support these assertions. Apart from some doubts about the grand strategic situation in the Mediterranean in January, his major concerns during the operational planning appear to have been the possible delay in starting the operation due to diversions of German forces into the Balkans, and his annoyance at Hitler's demand for an amendment to the General Staff's plan.

Hitler did not share his generals' conviction that the capture of Moscow would be decisive. Furthermore, he feared that in attempting to reach the city the generals would allow the campaign to deteriorate into a frontal advance which would merely push the Russians back. After the initial encirclement battles on the frontier, he preferred to swing the armoured spearhead north-east to envelop the Russians against the Baltic coast and secure Leningrad as a base for further operations. In the south similar operations could be conducted towards the Black Sea followed by an 'expedition' to seize the Caucasian oilfields. Neither Brauchitsch nor Halder agreed with Hitler's view, but, after long arguments like those which had attended Operation 'Yellow', they incorporated Hitler's thrust to-

Victorious German troops on a captured Russian locomotive

621

General Thomas, Head of the War Economy and Armaments Office in the OKW, and his staff

wards Leningrad into their directives and failed to conduct any serious planning for its implementation. The Caucasus expedition was ignored.

Just as the operational planning was completed and Halder was about to depart on two weeks' leave some details of the logistic planning were discussed. This was not unusual: in the German army the Quartermaster General was expected to meet the needs of the operations as best he could. Throughout the General Staff, supply and transport was regarded as the 'poor step-sister' of tactics. According to Hermann Teske, this weakness began in the *Kriegsakademie* where the instructors in this field

lacked instructional material and practical, up-to-date experience. There were few regulations on supply and none at all on transportation. Staff officers appointed as Ib on army or divisional staffs found that in practice the situation was no better. On mobilization some motor transport columns obtained vehicles from government departments or from civilian road haulage companies. The multiplicity of different vehicles created a nightmare for the repair and maintenance workshops. Major movements of troops and supplies were conducted by the railways.

The man who made the system work was General Rudolf Gercke, the Chief of Transportation on the General Staff. Gercke had suffered through illness and was almost a recluse. But between the wars he had gained considerable expertise in transportation systems in industry, and he combined great devotion to duty with an impressive memory for detail. Since July 1940 he had been working on the road and rail system to support a campaign in Russia, but he had warned Halder that there would be serious delays while the railway was extended beyond the Soviet border because the Russians used a broader gauge and every line would have to be adjusted to take German rolling stock. Meanwhile, the battling armies would have to depend upon road transport for an advance of 600 miles. On returning from leave, Halder called a meeting of senior administrators to explain the improvisations which this would cause. But the true seriousness of the situation was revealed when one of the generals present informed Halder that only fifty per cent of the army's tyre needs could be met, and that there was sufficient fuel oil only for the concentration of forces and two months of combat.

The man who presented this startling information was General Georg Thomas, Head of the War Economy and Armaments Office in the OKW. As the Reichswehr Ministry's economics expert, Thomas had welcomed the task of reviving Germany's war economy because he felt that the

Rumanian soldiers receive the Iron Cross from a German officer

Field-Marshals Brauchitsch and List
visit the Bulgarian War Minister,
General Daskaloff, in Sofia

power vacuum in central Europe between a strong Russia and the Western Powers was a 'threat to the
maintenance of peace'. Early in 1933,
before the end of the cooperation with
the Red Army, Thomas visited Russia.
On his return he warned Hitler that
friendly relations should be maintained with the Soviet Union because
'in a few years time it would become a
power of inestimable strength'. Hitler
flatly rejected his report because he
thought that Thomas and his colleagues had been deluded by a false
front. 'Bolshevism', he said, 'can never
be capable of constructive effort.'
These views shocked Thomas, who
became increasingly critical as he

watched Hitler's risky foreign and
rearmament policies develop. He was
convinced that Germany should rearm
'in depth' by building up her raw material sources, production and transport systems on a long-term basis. A
strong Germany would then be better
able to negotiate further revisions of
the Treaty of Versailles, especially
on the eastern border.

Hitler rejected this type of rearmament because it lacked policy aims
or deadlines for military action. He
preferred to stake all on gaining a
short lead in armaments and using it
to fight limited wars for 'living space'
while his enemies were still weak and
divided. The economic arguments of
Thomas, like the strategic arguments
of Beck, were irrelevant to Hitler.
What was the use of delaying the construction of the Panzer forces until

sources of fuel oil were secured if the only means of winning such sources was by rapid 'lightning wars'? By 1938 Thomas found his department subordinated to three superiors: the Head of the Four Year Plan Organisation, Göring, who shouted him down at meetings; the Minister of Economics, Walter Funk, who refused to do anything which 'might give the Führer the idea that he wished to influence him in his decisions'; and Keitel who thought Thomas was 'influenced by every pacifist who refused to recognise the Führer's greatness'. But even Keitel was sceptical about the possibility of defeating Russia with a single Blitzkrieg campaign and in August 1940 he urged Hitler to put the German economy on a total war footing as Thomas had suggested. Hitler refused, and as a result aircraft production declined, munition production fell short of the requirements for the coming campaign and the doubling of the Panzer and motorized forces was achieved only by reducing the tank strength of the Panzer divisions and using French vehicles with no cross-country capability.

In November Göring ordered Thomas to conduct a study of the effects of an operation against Russia on the war economy. The report made it clear that immediate economic relief would be felt if the Caucasian

A Greek general discusses surrender terms with a German officer

oilfields were captured intact, together with a large proportion of Russian road and rail transport, power stations, agricultural tractors and industrial plants. Furthermore, the population would have to be won over to collaboration. The whole image was so unrealistic that Thomas hoped it would convince the Nazi leaders that the conquest and exploitation of Russia was not feasible. But it had the opposite effect on Göring. Keitel, knowing that Hitler '. . . did not allow economic difficulties to influence his planning', probably gave it scant attention.

Meanwhile, Halder had gone to Brauchitsch with Thomas's dismal statistics. The Commander-in-Chief agreed that the purpose of 'Barbarossa' was not clear if it would neither improve Germany's war economic base nor strike Britain. He was also depressed by the defeats suffered by the Italians in North Africa and Greece which might afford the British the chance to open a front in the south while Germany was tied down in Russia. It was therefore decided that in addition to Operation 'Marita' in Greece, a support operation would be conducted in North Africa by a small mobile force under General Erwin Rommel.

Halder was annoyed by this diversion but he recognised that a major Italian defeat might have serious repercussions in the Balkans and expose the Rumanian oilfields to attack. Without Rumanian oil the Wehrmacht could not continue the war, and so it had been German policy to avoid any crisis or conflict in southeast Europe. In 1939 the Western Powers, wishing to avoid provoking Mussolini into the war, had limited themselves to sabotage against the oil barges on the Danube. Nevertheless, the Operations Branch of the German General Staff had developed plans for a swift operation in Rumania and defence of the oilfields should the need arise. *Abwehr* counter-espionage agents had been active in Rumania since 1939, and early in 1940 they began to work in cooperation with Rumanian security forces. Meanwhile, hoping to divert Russia away from the Balkans, General Jodl proposed that the Soviet Army should carry out a drive through Iraq and Iran towards the Persian Gulf. But in June 1940 when the Germans were fully committed in the West the Russians occupied Bessarabia and Northern Bukhovina. This blow, coming at the time of the Western Powers'

German paratroops execute Greek partisans on the island of Crete

117

defeat, forced Rumania to call upon Hitler for protection. This he granted on condition that the territorial claims of Hungary and Bulgaria were first met, and in October 1940 General Hansen's 'Military Mission', comprising motorized units of the army and fighter and flak formations of the Luftwaffe moved into Rumania, took over the country's defences and began to retrain and modernise the Rumanian Army '. . . in case a war with Russia is forced upon us'.

At the same time, without consulting the General Staff, Hitler attempted to set up an anti-British coalition in the Western Mediterranean. This failed, partly because Mussolini was so jealous of Hitler's action in Rumania that he decided to attack Greece. From this point on, German strategy in the Mediterranean was designed only to secure the 'soft underbelly' of Europe against British interference during the Russian campaign. Brauchitsch still felt that Germany should undertake a major campaign there to capture the Suez Canal and the oil of the Middle East before turning on Russia. Admiral Raeder shared this view, arguing that an attack on Russia from the Middle East would immediately deprive her of the Caucasian oilfields and thus cripple her war economy. Göring and Jodl also had similar ideas but they refused to press them on Hitler. The failure of the OKW to coordinate a Mediterranean strategy by bringing together the arguments of the three service chiefs doomed Germany to the fatal frontal assault on Russia. At the crucial moment in January 1941 the Army General Staff also failed to exert a strong influence, mainly because its chief, Halder preferred a direct assault either on Britain ·or Russia to an indirect strategy in the Mediterranean and the Balkans. But he was unable to prevent events from causing further diversion of effort and loss of time before 'Barbarossa' began. Throughout the winter diplomatic

attempts had been made to bring Yugoslavia into the Anti-Comintern Pact. Finally in March the Belgrade government decided to follow the example of Hungary, Rumania and Bulgaria, but it was promptly overthrown by a *coup d'état*. Hitler reacted with angry swiftness. He summoned the army and Luftwaffe Chiefs of Staff and ordered an extension of the forthcoming campaign in Greece to include Yugoslavia. On returning to Zossen Halder conferred with Brauchitsch, Paulus, Heusinger, Gercke and Wagner on the means of concentrating forces for this unexpected campaign. Later it was decided to postpone 'Barbarossa' from May until 22nd June to allow time for the nine divisions diverted to Yugoslavia to reassemble in Rumania and Poland. In fact, General Freiherr von Weichs conducted the campaign in Yugoslavia with such speed that his forces were back in the assembly areas for 'Barbarossa' by the end of May. In Greece the delay was longer and the wear and losses sustained by the Panzer divisions more serious.

The planning and conduct of the Balkan campaign also imposed a heavy strain on the General Staff. On 29th March General Paulus called a special conference in Vienna with Field-Marshal List and General von Greiffenberg (who had left the OKH to become Chief of Staff of Twelfth Army for the attack on Greece), and with Generals Freiherr von Weichs and von Kleist, whose Second Army and Panzer Group I had been given the task of attacking Yugoslavia. Paulus then went to Budapest to discuss Hungary's cooperation in the campaign. On 5th April Field-Marshal von Brauchitsch and General Halder accompanied by a detachment from the General Staff, set up a temporary headquarters at Wiener Neustadt from which to direct the campaign. Hitler moved his special train into a nearby tunnel, accompanied by a field echelon of the OKW's Section 'L'. As in Poland, the German victory in

Finland's Marshal Mannerheim with
Hitler and Keitel at the Führer's HQ

Yugoslavia was assured not only by
the material and tactical superiority
of the Wehrmacht, but also by the
strategic advantage of an attack coming from three directions. In Greece in
spite of the rough terrain, the Germans made imaginative use of their
mobile forces and air superiority and
quickly overwhelmed the Greek and
British defences. On 21st April the
Greek Army surrendered to SS
General Dietrich acting on behalf of
Field-Marshal List. But Mussolini
immediately protested that Italy
should have participated in the surrender negotiations. Hitler therefore
ordered an endorsement of the surrender with Italian participation. But
Field-Marshal List refused to humiliate an enemy who had fought bravely.
As a result General Jodl was flown to
Athens to preside over the charade.
    The Wehrmacht still had a further
task: the capture of Crete. The

The Finnish Chief of Staff,
General Heinrichs

119

General Staff was convinced that as long as the British held the island they would be able to maintain naval and air superiority in the eastern Mediterranean, and would have a base from which to mount landings on the Balkan coast or air attacks on the Rumanian oilfields. So the OKH agreed to provide General Ringel's 5th Mountain Division and part of the 6th to support the landings by paratroops of General Student's XI Air Corps. Although the island was won, the cost to XI Air Corps was high: 4,000 of the parachute troops killed and 350 aircraft, more than half of them transports, lost or damaged. As a result Hitler refused to commit this corps again to a major airborne attack.

Even as Halder left the temporary headquarters at Wiener Neustadt, he was reminded that he still had worries in the Mediterranean theatre. General Rommel, instead of stabilizing the Italian defences in Libya, was 'rushing all over the place with his widely strewn forces, launching probing attacks and splitting up his troops.' Having rejected the idea of going to Africa himself, Halder decided to send Paulus who knew Rommel personally and who seemed the only man on the General Staff able to influence this 'crazy soldier' who was 'in no way equal to his leadership responsibility'. Rommel was well aware that Paulus had come to restrain him. Instead of personally conducting him round, the 'Desert Fox' remained at his headquarters and sent his visitor off to the Tobruk front with only an adjutant to guide him. The methodical OQuI was appalled at Rommel's risky improvisations and on his return he recommended that the *Afrikakorps* should occupy defensive positions in which it could put its formations in order, replenish supplies, and guard the coast. Unfortunately for the British, Rommel ignored this advice which would have forced him to fight on their terms. By making his own rules

of desert warfare Rommel won himself a lasting reputation and even the begrudging respect of his enemies. But to Halder the North African campaign was a mere 'expedition' with a few divisions. By the third week of June his General Staff had completed the massive task of assembling almost 150 divisions on the Soviet borders.

The German deployment in the East was further complicated by the need to coordinate plans with Finland and Rumania. From the start of the planning Hitler had assumed that these countries would participate in the attack on Russia. Both had territory to regain, and both gave access to the Soviet Union. Furthermore, the Finnish nickel mines and Rumanian oilfields were essential to the German war economy and vulnerable to Russian counter-measures. Military cooperation with Rumania commenced when the German Military Mission arrived in the autumn of 1940. But the General Staff only began joint planning with the Finns when General Talvela visited Berlin in December 1940, and held preliminary discussions with Göring and Halder. In January the Finnish Chief of Staff, General Heinrichs, also visited Berlin, bringing answers to Halder's 'hypothetical' questions about Finland's capability should a conflict break out with Russia. In February 1941 the Chief of Staff of the Army of Norway, Colonel Buschenhagen, visited Helsinki and toured Northern Finland, paying particular attention to the problem of defending the nickel mines. In May General Heinrichs again arrived in Berlin and had talks with Jodl and Halder. Differences between German and Finnish aims and the fact that Falkenhorst's Army of Norway was directly subordinated to the OKW led to a complex command structure in Finland. In order to reduce these problems Halder sent General Waldemar Erfurth, formerly OQuV on the General Staff, to Mannerheim's headquarters as representative of the OKH and OKW, and Chief of

Liaison Staff North. By mid-June he had reached agreement with Marshal Mannerheim and General Heinrichs on the location and timing of the Finnish attacks. Meanwhile, the complicated assembly of troops in Lapland was under way. From the Arctic Ocean to the Black Sea the Wehrmacht stood ready for its greatest test.

On 22nd June 1941 over three million German soldiers crossed the Soviet border. They were organised into 149 divisions including 19 Panzer, 10 motorized, and 4 SS divisions. A further infantry division, two mountain divisions and an SS division were in Finland. The remaining 59 divisions were distributed between Scandinavia, the West, the Balkans and Africa. Not a single division remained in Germany. The command of these forces required headquarters for four army groups, thirteen armies, four Panzer groups, forty-six corps and twelve other staffs. In October 1940 a further general staff training course was started under the direction of Colonel Hermann Foertsch and an instructional staff of four lieutenant-colonels and four majors. Of the 99 members, 61 were appointed to the General Staff, 17 were allocated to further training, and 21 failed the course. The next course, between January and March had 108 members, 74 of which passed, 14 went to further training and 20 failed. In spite of the increase in the number of general staff appointments as a result of the expansion of the army for 'Barbarossa', these courses enabled the Central Branch to fill all vacancies and to set up a reserve of thirty staff officers. The expansion, organisation and equipping of this army of 208 divisions had been a difficult task for the General Staff. Six months earlier there were only 104 combat divisions; 26 were being formed and 18 still had their personnel on leave in industry or agriculture to reinforce the economy for the intensive period of production preceding the campaign. Nevertheless, throughout 1941 the output of munitions and army equipment (other than tanks) actually declined. In April 1941 Halder began to plan the reduction of the army to 144 divisions in the autumn after 'Barbarossa'. No further short general staff courses were considered necessary. A quick victory was expected. Brauchitsch was confident that the 'hard and bloody' frontier battles would last about four weeks and would be followed by a mopping-up operation against 'slight opposition'.

The initial successes seemed to confirm this optimism. The Russians appeared to be taken completely by surprise and suffered very heavy losses in the initial battles. In the great envelopment between Bialystok and Minsk, Army Group 'Centre' claimed to have taken 324,000 prisoners, and destroyed or captured 3,332 tanks and 1,809 guns by 11th July. In the slogging battle in the South Rundstedt claimed 150,000 prisoners, 1,970 tanks and 2,190 guns. Army Group 'North' accounted for 250,000 prisoners, 1,170 tanks and 3,075 guns. On 30th June Hitler told Halder that after reaching Smolensk in mid-July the infantry would take Moscow by August. Meanwhile, the Panzer forces could 'clean up' the Baltic states and then assemble east of Moscow for their next tasks. As it was Halder's birthday Hitler stayed for tea and, in an expansive mood, talked about the effect of Russia's defeat on European unity and on the willingness of states like Turkey and Afghanistan to cooperate with Germany.

Three days later the Chief of the General Staff also began to sketch out future plans based on Directive No 32 which the OKW had issued in 11th June. As soon as the Russian forces had been destroyed part of the Wehrmacht would continue operations against the Russian industrial centres. But the war against Britain would then take priority. Offensives would converge on the Middle East from Bulgaria via Turkey, from the Caucasus via Iran and from Libya across the Nile. Gibraltar would be taken and also the Spanish and Portuguese Atlantic coast (Operation 'Isabella'). But even as Halder was outlining these plans there was an angry scene between Hitler and Brauchitsch about the danger of Russian counterattacks from the Pripet Marshes on the flank of Rundstedt's thrust into the Ukraine. 'This concern is, of course, tactically not unjustified', noted Halder. 'But that is why we have army and corps commanders. At the top there is a lack of trust in the command apparatus which is one of the strongest aspects of our leadership. This is due to a failure to understand the strength resulting from the unified training and education of the leadership corps.'

Motorized German units receive a warm welcome in the Ukraine

Next day he expressed confidence that 'in all one may assume that the enemy has insufficient forces for a serious defence . . .' Colonel Kinzel of the Foreign Armies East Branch estimated that of 164 rifle divisions, 89 had been destroyed or badly mauled. Only 9 of the 29 tank divisions were still capable of combat.

The assessment of the performance of the various arms in the field was conducted by the Inspector Generals attached to the OKH. On 6th July General Ott, the Inspector General of Infantry told Halder that the 'morale and sense of superiority of the troops was everywhere very good. Fortunately the troops feel they have mastered the enemy tanks.' He described Russian attacks of 'up to twelve ranks deep without support from heavy weapons but with shouts of "Hurra" (and) unbelievable Russian losses.'

But gradually the tone of the reports began to change. The Russians seemed to find more replacements than expected. Meanwhile, losses and breakdowns had reduced the German mobile forces to fifty per cent strength. The infantry were showing signs of exhaustion. The supply situation was becoming serious. The advance was behind schedule; Smolensk had not fallen, there was little chance of capturing Moscow in August, and even less of reaching the Volga early in October or Baku and Batum at the beginning of November. Hitler became increasingly critical and meddled constantly in the direction of operations. On 25th July Halder told a meeting of the Chiefs of Staff of the Army Groups and Armies to treat 'Flank shots from the stratosphere' with a patient but swift response. He also advised the increasing use of front-line officers to report the situation to Hitler because they were 'more believed than we are!' Halder's concern for the future was reflected in his warning to the Chiefs of Staff to 'Give thought right now about winter problems!'

The realisation that time was running out made the Generals at the OKH and Army Group 'Centre' eager to concentrate on a drive for Moscow in the hope of forcing the Russians into a last decisive battle. But Hitler had never been convinced of Moscow's importance and ordered the Panzer groups to turn towards Leningrad and the Ukraine. The arguments which followed revived all the old tensions between Hitler and the OKH. Brauchitsch was again reduced to a

In the initial battles very heavy losses were suffered by the Russians

Hitler's favorite, Guderian *(left)* and
General Hoth

field-marshal was very depressed. He had already reported that 'unless the Russians soon collapse somewhere, the task of striking them down once and for all will become very difficult before the winter sets in.' The tension which resulted from this situation led Brauchitsch to relieve the OKH liaison officer to Guderian's Panzer Group of his appointment. Bock also requested Guderian's dismissal, but Brauchitsch agreed only to reprimand him for his selfwilled behaviour and for his lack of caution in making a request for reinforcements over the radio which might have been overheard by the OKW!

The conduct of the campaign was not the only cause of tension in the general staff corps in Russia. The Nazi policy towards the Slavs and the Jews also caused many officers to reconsider their attitudes towards Hitler. The army leaders were fully aware of the brutality and excesses of the SS in Poland, because the reports written by the indignant military commander, General Blaskowitz, were circulated among the staffs in the West by Colonel Groscurth and others who were determined to ensure that no senior officer could claim ignorance. Nevertheless, some still managed to convince themselves that the atrocities were the result of indiscipline in the storm-troops' ranks rather than the deliberate policy of the state. In Russia such self-delusion was no longer possible. Even before the campaign, on 30th March 1941, Hitler told two hundred senior officers that the 'criminal' communist leadership and Slavic intelligentsia would be exterminated. Only Bock protested at the orders for shooting of partisans and commissars and refused to issue them to his army group. But the field-marshal's action was a feeble compromise in the eyes of his brother-in-law, Henning von Tresckow, who was

state of hopeless resignation. Halder was 'beside himself' with anger, but he doggedly refused to give up until Hitler's favourite, General Guderian, made a final presentation of the case for the capture of Moscow. However, the Panzer general soon realized that the Führer would not be persuaded so, although he had described the diversions southward as 'a crime' to Bock and Halder the day before, he now agreed that his entire Panzer group should be turned south towards Kiev. Afterwards when he reported his change of mind to Halder the Chief of the General Staff 'suffered a complete nervous collapse'. After hurling criticism at Guderian, he phoned Bock and complained to him. The

German troops are instructed to shoot civilians attempting to leave Leningrad

Ia on his staff, and his adjutants, Graf Hans von Hardenberg and Graf Heinrich von Lendorff. These men watched with horror as Himmler's *Einsatzgruppen* followed the advancing armies and began to round up thousands of victims for the slaughter. Tresckow repeatedly tried to persuade Bock to act against Hitler. Finally the ambitious field-marshal turned on his persecutor and angrily told him that he was not a 'South American operetta general', and he 'would not tolerate attacks on the Führer'. In November, however, Bock raised the subject of the *Einsatzgruppen* with Halder when he discovered that train loads of Jews were being brought from Germany into his Army Group rear area for execution. The use of these trains he protested must reduce the number available for supplying the Army Group.

In October Bock had his chance to secure the place he wanted in history by inflicting a decisive defeat on the Russians. Most of the Panzer forces were redeployed under his command for a triple-pronged thrust towards Moscow. The great double envelopment battle of Viasma-Briansk yielded 663,000 prisoners. Together with the 665,000 taken at Kiev a month earlier this seemed to represent a total loss which no army could survive. Bock noted in his diary that the tens of thousands of prisoners made a

'ghastly' impression. 'Completely fatigued and half starving, these unfortunates stumble (to Smolensk) Many collapse dead or exhausted on the roadside . . . there is no help for them.' Nevertheless, he did find time to write a vigorous protest to Brauchitsch that the SS 'Special Commandos' were trespassing on the army's jurisdiction when they went into the POW camps to select prisoners for execution. As far as the prisoners were concerned the only difference was that the SS gave them a quicker death. In November Halder recorded the 'horrible impression' made by the thousands dying of cholera and starvation in POW camps. But this was all part of the Nazi policy towards the Slavs. In the north, where Leningrad was now surrounded, the troops were told to shoot civilians if they attempted to get out because it was hoped that some two million people would starve to death there before the city was finally levelled.

Similar plans were made for Moscow, but were not fulfilled. The claws of the Panzer armies failed to close. Bock's exhausted troops bogged down in mud and snow. When General Zhukhov counterattacked in December there were no German reserves to stabilize the front. The field-marshal reported sick and went home. But the main scapegoat for the failure in Russia was the mentally and physically exhausted Commander-in-Chief, Field-Marshal von Brauchitsch.

Totaler Krieg

Field-Marshal von Brauchitsch suffered a heart attack on 10th November, and on 7th December he offered his resignation. In September 1939 he had agreed with Halder that if a resignation became necessary they should leave office together. But now he urged Halder to remain as Chief of the General Staff because only he could help to control the disastrous situation on the Russian front. Furthermore, it seemed likely that the ambitious and volatile Field-Marshal von Reichenau would at last be appointed Commander-in-Chief. If this occurred Halder would be needed to maintain stability and confidence in the OKH. The Chief of Staff was not sorry to hear Brauchitsch's decision. He had become a little more than 'a letter carrier between the OKH and Hitler', and finding Halder critical of his accounts of his conversations with Hitler he became increasingly uncommunicative and ineffective. Hitler referred to his Commander-in-Chief as 'that man of straw', but for days he refused to accept his resignation. Then on the 19th December he announced that '. . . anybody can exer-

cise that little bit of operational leadership. The task of the Commander-in-Chief is to educate the army in National Socialism. I know of no general who can fulfil this task to my satisfaction. I have therefore decided to take over the command of the army myself.'

The OKH was now to be confined to the direction of operations on the Russian front. Field-Marshal Keitel took over all Brauchitsch's administrative functions and the OKW became responsible for the control of all other theatres of war. But this did not reduce Halder's work load. Since September 1939 he had conferred with Hitler on fifty-four occasions, an average of less than twice a month. Now he was required to attend Hitler's daily conferences. This involved much preparation, an hour's drive each way between HQ OKH at Angerburg to the Führer HQ *Wolfsschanze*, near Rastenburg, and the time spent, often in frustrating argument, over Hitler's

Before the collapse of the German army; high-spirited troops in Stalingrad with knocked out Russian T34 tank

128

A pause in the street fighting: Russian counterattacks begin to wear down German morale

Lieutenant-General Reinhard Gehlen, in 1942 Head of the Foreign Armies East Section

map table. Outwardly, the daily meetings of the senior members of the OKH and OKW seemed to achieve a union of the two factions in the General Staff. But in fact the schism was not widened.

The difficulty lay mainly in the contempt which Halder felt for Keitel and Jodl. The Chief of the OKW was a man who would never have risen to the level of a corps chief of staff but for the fact that he was an abnormally hard worker and an abjectly willing subordinate. When Halder succeeded Beck in 1938 Keitel was still loyal to the General Staff and accepted criticisms of the OKW in good humour. He even warned Halder of some of Hitler's ideas. But during the quarrels of the winter of 1939–40 he dissociated himself from the OKH. After the war Halder claimed that he held several private interviews with Keitel in order to convince him that his servility to Hitler was undignified. There were 'tears, and assurances that he only acted for the best, but not the slightest attempt to straighten his

spine'. By 1942 Keitel had become 'intriguing and down-right wicked' in his endeavours to identify with his Führer and to protect him from disturbing or unpleasant news.

Halder regarded Jodl as a man of greater character and military ability than Keitel. As his instructor on the staff course in Munich in 1922-3 Halder had assessed Jodl clever but over-ambitious. His overestimation of himself 'was unfortunately encouraged during his first years in the OKH, and it was with relief that he was "unloaded" on the newly formed OKW'. Jodl's enthusiasm for the for-mation of a Wehrmacht General Staff only increased the hostility for him in the OKH. His unconcealed admiration for Hitler was also repugnant to the General Staff. In August 1941 Jodl shocked Halder by admitting that though he could not fault the argument for an attack on Moscow, he still felt that the Führer was right because he had 'a sixth sense'.

Halder was also uncomfortably aware that there was a strong faction in the OKW which was still actively working against Hitler in spite of the lack of support they had found in the OKH. Hitherto, Halder's dealings with the OKW had been mainly conducted through General Warlimont. But now his Section 'L' had its own campaigns to conduct in the Mediterranean and Scandinavia so Halder found himself in less congenial company for the difficult tasks facing him in the final stage of his career at the head of the General Staff.

When it became unlikely that Russia would be defeated before the onset of winter, Halder and Colonel von Ziehlberg had decided to resume the short staff courses to meet the two hundred vacancies on the General Staff which had occurred through the further expansion of the Army and through losses, including nine killed and many sick and wounded. Major General Weckmann, formerly Chief of Staff of the Ninth Army who was recovering from a wound, was placed in charge, and given Lieutenant-Colonel Walther Wenck and six other experienced staff officers as instructors. The course took place between the end of March and 9th May 1942. Fifty of the sixty students passed the course. The 59 officers on the next course were trained by attachment to various corps headquarters. After that courses combined a fourteen-week attachment with eight weeks of classroom training. Most of the new staff officers went as Ibs to divisions in Russia.

The German army experienced its first major defeat on the eastern front

in the winter of 1941-2. The supply system broke down. The men lacked winter clothing, shelter and fuel. There were insufficient munitions, foodstuffs and equipment replacements. In the course of Zhukhov's offensive 3,500 artillery pieces and eleven thousand machine guns were abandoned or destroyed. Between December and March 723,200 men were lost, but only 336,00 were available as replacements. The General Staff worked vigorously to improvise defensive plans. But a complete collapse was averted mainly by Hitler's decision not to attempt a major withdrawal, by the tactical skill of field commanders like Küchler, Kluge, Hoth and Model, who had replaced Leeb, Bock, Stülpnagel and Strauss, and by the training and discipline of the troops themselves. The Russians also helped by failing to concentrate their effort against specific objectives until the spring. By then the Germans had recovered sufficiently to mount strong counterattacks in the Crimea and at Kharkhov, where Field-Marshal von Bock had taken over Army Group 'South' in place of Reichenau, who had died of a heart attack. As the new commander of Reichenau's Sixth Army Hitler selected General Paulus. But Bock complained to Halder that he was 'not equal to his task, looked on the black side, underestimated his own troops, and, in short, lacked spirit'. He was, Bock added, a 'methodical man' but if he stayed he should have a new Chief of Staff. Halder agreed that General Heim was somewhat 'eccentric' and decided to replace him with General Arthur Schmidt. Later the army group command was also changed. Bock retained Army Group 'South' with the Second, Sixth and Fourth Panzer Armies, and Sodenstern as his Chief of Staff. A new Army Group 'A' was formed under Field-Marshal List, with von Greiffenberg as Chief of Staff, to control Seventeenth and First Panzer Armies.

The offensive by these army groups on the southern sector had been decided upon by Hitler because he believed that the capture of the oil of the Caucasus would lead to a collapse of the Soviet war economy and would also enable Germany to launch operations against the British oil supply in the Middle East. General Günther Blumentritt, the new OQuI, told Sir Basil Liddell Hart after the war that the General Staff was unable to assess the validity of Hitler's strategy because it was not represented at conferences on economic questions. The General Staff was doubtful about the chances of success when so much depended upon new inexperienced divisions and the flank protection on the Don provided by Italian, Hungarian and Rumanian formations.

These concerns and Halder's warnings about the strength and economic capacity of the Russians were brusquely rejected by Hitler. However, the Chief of Staff was determined that the colossal underestimation of the Russians, which had been one of the Germans' worst mistakes in 1941, should not be repeated. It was for this reason that he had decided to replace Kinzel in the Foreign Armies East Section with Gehlen. Lieutenant-Colonel Reinhard Gehlen was a cold, remorseless, industrious and ambitious staff officer. Between 1936 and 1939 he worked under Manstein, first in the Operations Section then at the headquarters of the Army Group 'South'. In the winter of 1939-40 he performed important studies for the Fortification Section. During the campaign in France he served as OKH liaison officer to Generals Busch and Hoth and, later, Guderian. When the Operations Branch was reorganised under Colonel Heusinger, Gehlen was selected to head Group I (East) and conduct the detailed planning for Operations 'Marita' and 'Barbarossa'. Heusinger reported him as 'an exemplary general staff officer. Personality,

Walter Schellenberg, who established
the *Sicherheitsdienst* in 1942

Bock's replacement, General Weichs

Field-Marshal Kesselring

knowledge and diligence far above average. Excellent sense of foresight and perception in operational matters. Completely reliable. Suitable for appointment as chief of staff of a corps or head of a department (on the General Staff).'

In the course of Operation 'Barbarossa' Halder sent Gehlen to the front as a representative of the General Staff. In July he was at the headquarters of Army Group 'North' and ill mid-August he toured the Finnish 'ont. He was very impressed by the rformance of Marshal Manner-

heim's soldiers who had willingly joined Hitler's 'crusade against Bolshevism' in the hope of regaining the territory lost to Russia in the Winter War, 1939–40. Finland's fight as Germany's ally in the North encouraged in Gehlen the idea that the Baltic peoples, the Ukrainians and White Russians might also be willing to fight against Stalin's regime if given the proper encouragement. On returning to HQ OKH Gehlen became immersed in the plans and improvisations by which the campaign was continued into the winter. On 1st April 1942 Halder told him that he would take Kinzel's place as Head of the Foreign Armies East Section. Ie was a good choice. In contrast to the easy going Kinzel, Gehlen had the right methodical, calculating mind for the assessment of intelligence. His main liability was the obsessive hatred for Communism which at times affected his judgement.

Shortly after Gehlen assumed his new duties Halder told him that daily intelligence summaries as produced by Kinzel giving the location and strength of enemy formations, were no longer adequate. He also required long-term assessments of Russian intentions which would be issued every four to eight weeks. Gehlen had long felt that intelligence work had been seriously neglected in the General Staff. At the *Kriegsakademie* instruction was limited to the collection and evaluation of tactical information on the divisional front, plus a few lectures on espionage. During the period of *Blitzkrieg* victories there had been little need for more than assessments of the immediate situation. Now, in order to stress the importance of intelligence, Gehlen persuaded Halder and Colonel von Ziehlberg, Chief of the Central Section responsible for appointment of general staff officers, that the Ic (intelligence officers) on formation headquarters should be of the same rank as the Ia (operations officer). He also reorganized his section. Group I under Major Heinz Danko Herre continued to produce the daily intelligence digest based on reports from the three army group fronts, and Major Kühlein's Group II worked on the long-term reports. Group III contained the Russian experts, mostly Baltic Germans or Germans born in Russia. Their main tasks were translating Russian documents and military manuals, interrogating prisoners and evaluating material. This group was headed by Captain Petersen, but Gehlen's Ia, Lieutenant-Colonel Freiherr Alexis von Roenne exercised personal direction over its work.

Further improvements in use of intelligence were made by extending the collaboration between the Foreign Armies East Section and the *Abwehr*. Colonel Piekenbrock's Group I (Espionage) collected information but the *Abwehr* lacked the means to analyse it. Admiral Canaris therefore agreed to improve the delivery of all reports of value to Gehlen's section. *Abwehr* Control Station 'Walli I' was moved from the Warsaw area to a site only 20 miles from HQ OKH at Angerburg. Within less than a month the improvements justified themselves. Using the reports from the front, Gehlen told Halder that the Russians had shifted considerable force to the southern sector, but he could not predict how they intended to use it. Then, on 30th April an *Abwehr* report revealed that a member of the Soviet Central Committee had told the editor of *Pravda* that the *Stavka* (Soviet Supreme Staff) had decided to mount a spoiling offensive in May. Thus Timoshenko's offensive at Kharkhov did not take the General Staff by surprise and Bock's counterattacks resulted in the envelopment of the Russian thrust.

Gehlen's work was not limited to the Russian front. His section was responsible for intelligence on the Balkan and Scandinavian countries, and was also called upon to report on the war potential and probable intentions of the United States. Later, Foreign Armies East dealt only with the flow of American equipment to Russia, and left the American war effort to the *Abwehr* and its rival, the foreign intelligence section of the *Sicherheitsdienst* which was developed by Walter Schellenberg in 1942.

The improvements in the General Staff's intelligence system resulting from Gehlen's appointment were overshadowed by a serious breach of security when the Ia of the 23rd Panzer Division crash-landed near the Russian lines with a marked map and an outline of the operational plan o XXXX Panzer Corps' role in the ma summer offensive. Since Hitler h

The Allied landing at Dieppe is successfully repulsed

ordered that operational plans should be passed on verbally, the subsequent court martial condemned the corps and division commanders to prison. Göring and Bock managed to persuade Hitler to remit the sentences, but the incident provided him with a further excuse for heaping abuse on the general staff corps. Paulus, mortified by these events in his Sixth Army, reported that he was instituting court martial proceedings against himself. But Bock impatiently told him to 'Keep his nose pointed towards the front'.

Nevertheless further leadership crises followed as the offensive developed. Bock, accused of an unnecessary diversion of Panzer divisions into Voronezh, was replaced by Weichs. When Halder criticised Hitler for doing the same thing at Rostov he provoked an outburst of rage. Early in September Hitler sent Jodl to find out why List's forces were not making better progress in the Caucasus and why he had refused to drop parachute troops on Tuapse. Jodl reported that List lacked sufficient forces to do better and that the paratroops would be lost if dropped beyond the reach of the over-extended ground forces. Hitler angrily refused to accept Jodl's report and reprimanded him for not enforcing the order. Jodl had reached the end of his tether. He resentfully quoted Hitler's own orders which had led to the over-extension of Army Group 'A'. Hitler was astounded that his most trusted general should make such an accusation. 'You're lying', he screamed and rushed out into the night. From then on instead of sitting with Keitel and Jodl in the mess Hitler ate alone. He ordered that every word at his situation conferences was to be taken down in shorthand. He also announced his intention of replacing Keitel and Jodl with Kesselring and Paulus, but later changed his mind. However, Field-Marshal List was dismissed, and Halder was warned that he too would soon go. The Chief of Staff took leave of the Führer after the daily conference on 24th September. Afterwards he made the final entry in his notebook: 'My nerves are worn out and his too are no longer fresh. We must part. [Hitler spoke of] the need to educate the General Staff in a fanatical belief in the idea [of National Socialism]. Determination to impose his will upon the Army also.' When Halder departed General Schmundt remarked, 'The last dam has now been breached and the spirit of the falsely trained General Staff can now be replaced with the spirit of Adolf Hitler.'

During his last days as Chief of the General Staff Halder gave, in Albert Speer's opinion, 'a rather hapless impression'. His successor, Lieutenant-General Kurt Zeitzler, 'was just the opposite: a straightforward, insensitive person who made his reports in a loud voice.' Hitler hoped he had found the sort of dynamic assistant he needed who 'doesn't go off and brood on my orders, but energetically sees to carrying them out.' Thus he had avoided Halder's contemporaries like Sodenstern, Salmuth, Greiffenberg and Manstein and picked this relatively junior staff officer, who in 1939 had stood 98th on the General Staff List. Zeitzler had first come to Hitler's notice in 1938 when as senior Army Staff Officer in Section 'L' of the OKW he had supplied statistics on the Czech defences. In 1940, when Kleist, a conservative cavalry general, was given command of the Panzer Group which was to launch the crucial blow across the Meuse, the vigorous Zeitzler was made his Chief of Staff. The success of Panzer Group 'Kleist' in the West and in the Balkans enhanced Zeitzler's reputation. As a result, when a new Chief of Staff was sought for the C-in-C West to 'shake up' the coastal defences Schmundt had little difficulty in securing the post for his friend Zeitzler. He tackled his new task with characteristic vigour, and when the Canadian landing at Dieppe was successfully repulsed he became the prime candidate for Halder's post.

On taking up his appointment Zeitzler decided to 'simplify' the General Staff and abolished the post of OQuI and sent General Blumentritt to take over the appointment he had vacated in the West. He also caused some dismay when he assembled the officers of the OKH and told them bluntly that he had no use on the General Staff for anybody who did not believe in the Führer and his method of command. On 3rd November 1942 he addressed the trainees on the seventh General Staff Course in similar terms. But Zeitzler himself soon had difficulty in upholding his own standards of loyalty. After long consultations with Gehlen he concluded that the Axis forces in Russia were dangerously over-extended, especially on the Don where the Russians were concentrating opposite the sectors held by Rumanian, Hungarian and Italian armies. But Hitler brushed aside his reports and refused to break off the attacks upon Stalingrad and the Caucasus. The best Zeitzler could do was to place an under-equipped Panzer corps in reserve behind the threatened Don front and add German anti-tank units to the Hungarian and Rumanian divisions. Special liaison groups containing signals unit and German general staff officers were attached to non-German formation headquarters. These inadequate measures added a further burden to the General Staff, which, according to Zeitzler 'from the most senior departmental chief to the most junior captain, shared my apprehension to the full and anxiously awaited the Russian attack which we all knew was imminent.' Even Ludwig Beck in retirement was kept informed of the dangerous situation on the Eastern Front. Colonel Groscurth now serving with a German infantry division with a Rumanian corps on the Don wrote to him describing the shortage of men, spare parts for vehicles, and weapons, especially artillery and anti-tank guns. Thus, while Hitler boasted of the triumphs of the Wehrmacht on the Volga and in Africa, an atmosphere of foreboding permeated the general staff corps.

In November the Russian counterblows fell exactly as expected, smashing the Rumanian armies, enveloping the Sixth Army in the ruined city of Stalingrad. Paulus, ever cautious in his actions, was now paralysed by his inability to decide whether loyally to obey his Führer's command to stand fast, or, like Rommel at El Alamein a month earlier, save the remnant of his army by breaking out of the trap. Colonel Helmuth Groscurth was among the 92,000 men captured. He died two months later.

Russian counter-blows fall on Stalingrad resulting in the surrender of the German Sixth army

The Last Act

A few days after Paulus surrendered to the Russians Gehlen wrote a memorandum in which he stated that 'For the sake of history it must be recorded here that . . . the General Staff was adamant that only the immediate withdrawal of the Sixth Army could save it from annihilation . . .' The Russians, he lamented, 'have applied standard German command principles: Zhukhov as military commander enjoys complete freedom within the framework of the task assigned to him; the Russians have adopted German tactics and . . . strategic doctrines. In the meantime we have borrowed from the Russians their earlier system of rigidly laying down the law on virtually everything and going into the tiniest details . . . German military leaders who can think and act independently are discouraged – indeed both such qualities

can lead to court martial . . . We have become benumbed, and are incapable of strategic action . . . But Gehlen was careful to record that 'It is not within the scope of this survey to discuss the reasons why these errors were nonetheless made.'

Not all the officers of the General Staff were as circumspect as Gehlen. Anger against Hitler's direction of the war aroused the spirit of revolt. At 'Army Group Centre' Tresckow at last found sufficient support to plan the assassination of Hitler. But the attempt, which took place when Hitler visited Kluge's headquarters in March 1943, miscarried because the bomb which Tresckow managed to get onto the Führer's aircraft failed to explode. In the West the conspirators gathered round General von Stülpnagel, the Military Governor of France, Colonel Finckh, the Quarter-

master West, and Lieutenant-Colonel Hofacker. In the Home Army General Olbricht, Head of the General Army Office, and later his chief of staff, Colonel Claus von Stauffenberg, added their support to Canaris and Oster in Berlin. In the OKH General Stieff, Head of the Organisation Section, General Fellgiebel, Inspector General of Signals, and Colonel von Roenne, Gehlen's deputy, who later became Head of Foreign Armies West, together with many of their subordinates, joined the plotters. Ludwig Beck remained the central source of inspiration. Few indeed in the general staff corps were unaware of what was going on. Most of those who were kept in ignorance were members of Hitler's immediate military entourage, who lived in prison-like conditions deep within the 'Wolf's Lair' at Rastenburg. In addition to Keitel, Jodl and

Planning the last act: General Ruoff, Hitler, Zeitzler, Generals Kleist and Kempf

Zeitzler, they included Schmundt, Scherff and Buhle. Schmundt took over the Army Personnel Office in the autumn of 1942 and persuaded Hitler that if he wanted to control the general staff corps the Central Section of the Army General Staff should be made part of the Personnel Office. Zeitzler protested in vain at the loss of his control over the members of the general staff. But this was not all, the post of OQuV was abolished and the former historical section and archives of the General Staff of the army were now delivered into the hands of Colonel Scherff, who was appointed 'Commissioner to the Führer for Military History.' His main task was to document Hitler's

Estonian civilians crowd around their German liberators

Field-Marshal Paulus, commander of the Sixth Army, surrenders at Stalingrad

military genius. More insidious still was the appointment of General Buhle as 'Head of the Army Staff on the OKW', a function which further split the General Staff and added to the confusion at the top.

The great majority of the general staff corps neither actively supported nor opposed the plotters in their ranks. They continued to hope that a victory could be won which would put an end to the 'wartime abnormalities' and restore stability and decency to Europe. A considerable number of leading general staff officers were convinced that the key to victory lay in persuading the Russian people to join the 'anti-Bolshevik

crusade'. In the Ukraine, the Baltic States and Caucasus elements of the population had welcomed the Germans as liberators. In Smolensk a committee of citizens asked Bock to allow them to set up a government and raise an army to fight Stalin. When this offer was rejected by Hitler von Bock suggested the recruitment of 200,000 Russian auxiliaries. Brauchitsch agreed but dared not voice the idea to Hitler. When Bock succeeded Reichenau, he found among the dead field-marshal's papers a memorandum suggesting a policy of cooperation and the raising of a Ukrainian army. He sent it to the OKH but nothing more was heard on the subject. Meanwhile many German formations had taken matters into their own hands and recruited thousands of *Hilfswillige*, volunteer non-combatant auxiliaries, mainly from the prisoner of war camps where hundreds of thousands were dying of starvation and disease. Meanwhile, a suitable leader for a 'Russian national liberation army' was found in the person of General Andrei Vlassov, who was captured on the Volkhov front. Colonel von Roenne and Captain Strik-Strikfeld of Gehlen's Group III managed to recruit a Russian staff to support him, and in the spring of 1943 he visited some of the 176 battalions and 38 independent companies which had been raised on the Eastern Front. General Ernst Köstring, former German Military Attaché in Moscow, was nominally in command of these volunteer units, and it was hoped that they could be formed into an army led by Vlassov. But when Keitel heard that the Russian general had been delivering nationalistic speeches to these troops he immediately ordered his return to a prisoner of war camp. Hitler later told Zeitzler that 'wrong ideas' about the Russian independence must be prevented. Thus the hopes of achieving a victory in Russia with Russian help were doomed by Hitler's fanatical racial policies.

Much hope was also aroused by the greatly increased war production achieved after Albert Speer was appointed Minister of Armaments and Munitions and the German economy was at last put on a total war footing. But, in spite of the remarkable rise in the numbers of aircraft, tanks and other weapons, German industry could not compete with the overwhelming quantities of war materials produced by the United States, Great Britain and Russia. As Beck and Thomas had long warned, Germany lacked sufficient fuel oil to run a modern war. Supplies from Rumania were insufficient, and after the defeat at Stalingrad the German armies had been forced to give up even their partial hold on the oil fields of the Caucasus. The opportunity to seize the oil of the Middle East had been lost when Hitler decided to commit the Wehrmacht to Operation 'Barbarossa' in 1941.

Even more illusory was the hope placed in new 'wonder weapons'. Since 1937 the army had been developing rocket missiles in a secret experimental station at Peenemünde on the Baltic. On 23rd March 1939 Brauchitsch and General Karl Becker, Head of the Army Weapons Office, had brought Hitler to see the rockets undergoing tests, But to the disappointment of General Dornberger and Werner von Braun, the leading military and scientific exponents of rockets, Hitler was sceptical of their military value, and in November he

Leading scientific proponents of rockets: *far left*, General Dornberger and *far right*, Werner von Braun

General Andrei Vlassov, leader of the 'Russian National Liberation Army' inspects his troops

Albert Speer, Minister of Armaments and Munitions

cut the budget for Peenemünde. Only with the secret support of Brauchitsch and Albert Speer was Dornberger able to keep work going. In 1942 Speer, Field-Marshal Milch and the armaments chiefs of the services went to Peenemünde and became convinced that rockets should go into mass production. But it was not until July 1943 that they won Hitler's support, and then Peenemünde was visited by the leaders of the OKW, the OKH and SS who all became eager to share the credit for the new weapon. In retrospect Speer admitted that the V-2 rocket was a 'mistaken investment'. It would have been better to have produced the 'Waterfall' anti-aircraft rocket which von Braun had also designed for use against the massive bomber forces operating over Germany day and night.

Meanwhile, Zeitzler and most of the general staff corps placed their hopes in well-tried mobile operations. Encouraged by the successful counter-attack launched by Manstein at Kharkhov in March 1943, Zeitzler proposed the use of all available Panzer divisions in an offensive designed to

A V-2 rocket is launched from Peenemünde

cut off the Soviet forces in the Kursk salient. He was strongly criticised by General Guderian who had been appointed Inspector General of Panzer Troops in February. (Much to Zeitzler's annoyance he was not subordinated to the General Staff but directly under Hitler.) But in spite of Guderian's arguments for a period of recuperation and re-equipping Hitler could not resist the temptation to launch the attack. The operation proved a costly failure and wasted valuable armoured formations needed in the defensive battles not only in Russia but also in Italy.

Meanwhile, the increase in casualties among staff officers led to a tripling of the number of trainees on staff courses in 1943. After March the courses were again at the *Kriegsakademie* in Berlin, and extended to six months duration. Part of this time was spent on attachment to a formation staff on one of the many fronts of 'Fortress Europe'.

As the pressures on the OKW theatres of war in the Mediterranean, the Balkans, the West and Norway increased, serious rivalry developed between Zeitzler and Jodl for the allocation of personnel and material. Zeitzler felt himself to be at a disadvantage, especially after the failure of the Kursk offensive. He met Guderian and Speer and suggested that attempts should be made to persuade Hitler to appoint a new Commander-in-Chief of the Army or an effective Wehrmacht Chief of Staff in place of Keitel. Manstein was agreed as the best choice, but nobody could convince Hitler of this. As Guderian later admitted 'their characters were too opposed'. Drastic changes in the high command finally did take place in July 1944. But these did not restore power to the army. On the contrary, they resulted from the bomb smuggled into Hitler's conference room by Colonel Claus von Stauffenberg. The explosion failed to kill Hitler but its aftermath shattered the General Staff.

General Zeitzler was not implicated in the assassination attempt on 20th July 1944. Nevertheless, Hitler immediately dismissed him because it was under his leadership that the General Staff had committed this ultimate act of treason. General Buhle, Hitler's first choice for the post of Chief of the General Staff, was injured by the explosion, and so Guderian was selected to be 'acting Chief of Staff of the Army'. The Panzer

Mussolini and Hitler examine the damaged conference room at Rastenburg

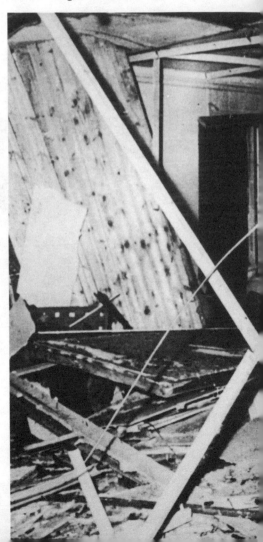

154

general was met by Keitel, Jodl and General Wilhelm Burgdorf, successor to Schmundt who was dying of his injuries. They told him that most of the officers of the OKH would have to be replaced. Some were wounded by the explosion, others were involved in the plot and most of the rest were packed off by Guderian because 'they had never seen the front'.

Guderian also made changes in the structure of the OKH. He appointed General Wenck Chief of the OKH Command Staff. His role was similar to that of the OQuI, controlling the Operations, Organisation and Foreign Armies East Sections. The Head of the Operations Section, Heusinger, was replaced by von Bonin. General Wagner, the Quartermaster-General, committed suicide and was succeeded by Colonel Toppe. The Inspector General of Signals, Erich Fellgiebel, was arrested and later executed; his

successor was General Praun. Of the senior officers on the OKH Guderian retained only 'the excellent General Gercke' and 'the reliable Colonel Gehlen'.

In Berlin the army's command structure was also shattered by the abortive plot. Generals Fromm, Olbricht, Stieff, Stauffenberg and their staffs were all either dead or under arrest. Beck, von Stülpnagel, von Kluge, von Tresckow and many others committed suicide. Rommel was persuaded to do so by General Burgdorf acting on Hitler's instructions. Field-Marshal von Witzleben, Colonel-General Höpner, General von Hase and over sixty general staff officers were arrested.

Hitler's hatred of the General Staff was such that at first he had wanted to disband it as an institution and suspend training of new general staff officers. Guderian succeeded in dissuading him from this course. Instead, further to humiliate the officer corps, Hitler formed a 'Court of Honour' presided over by Field-Marshal von Rundstedt, with Field-Marshal Keitel and Generals Guderian, Schroth, Kriebel and Kirchheim as members. Their task was to decide which officers should be brought to trial for complicity or fore-knowledge of the plot, and recommend their discharge from the Wehrmacht. The loss of many staff officers, including 24 hanged and 16 suicides, added to the heavy casualties suffered by the General Staff, which by the end of 1944 reached 166 killed, 10 sick, 143 missing. The bitterness of the situation was sharpened by the knowledge that in Russian POW camps many officers, including Field-Marshal Paulus, had joined the National Committee 'Free Germany' or the German Officers Association led by General Walther von Seydlitz-Kurzbach, and were writing anti-Nazi leaflets which the Russians

A prisoner of war compound housing German troops captured in the Ruhr pocket

dropped over German lines.

In addition to conducting the purge of the General Staff, Guderian also endured endless arguments with Hitler and his cronies on the conduct of the last hopeless battles of the war. He saw brave but ill-equipped troops placed under the command of SS Reichsführer Heinrich Himmler, who had neither military training nor experience. At the same time competent officers were demoted when their shattered units failed to meet the unrealistic demands made by Hitler over the map table. Hot-tempered at the best of times, Guderian frequently appalled Keitel by shouting back at Hitler. The gentlemanly Colonel Schmundt was no longer there to restore calm, and his successor, the oafish Burgdorf, only added to the acrimony. Guderian's health was suffering; he had high blood pressure and a heart ailment. Finally, on 28th March 1945, provoked by Hitler's unwarranted accusations against the troops and their commander in the hopeless battle at Küstrin, Guderian lost control of his anger. He was replaced by Lieutenant-General Hans Krebs, who had been Chief of Staff to Field-Marshal Model and then to Himmler as Commander of Army Group Vistula. He was present at the final macabre scenes in the Führer's bunker, and witnessed Hitler's final criticism of the General Staff. In a last message to Keitel Hitler complained that the generals had misdirected the Wehrmacht, 'resisted his strategy, undermined his policy, and conspired against his person . . . Disloyalty and betrayal have undermined resistance throughout the war. It was therefore not granted to me to lead the people to victory. The Army General Staff cannot be compared with the General Staff in the First World War. Its achievements were far behind those of the fighting front.'

During the night after Hitler's suicide General Krebs emerged from the bunker and entered the Soviet lines to negotiate a cease-fire. When asked to give up his pistol he refused, informing the Russians that 'A courageous opponent is allowed to keep his weapons during negotiations'. He was taken to General Vassili Chuikov, defender of Stalingrad, now Commander of the 8th Guards Army, who flatly refused anything but unconditional surrender. After arguing through the night Krebs returned to the bunker and, together with General Burgdorf, committed suicide. Before he died in the ruins of Berlin he doubtless recalled the occasion only four years earlier, when, as acting German Military Attaché in Moscow, he had been hugged by Stalin and told 'We will remain friends with you in any event'.

A few days later the Wehrmacht in the Schleswig-Holstein area surrendered to Field-Marshal Montgomery. General Eberhard Kinzel signed on behalf of the German army. Like Krebs, he shot himself shortly after. On 7th May a weeping Jodl signed the unconditional surrender at Rheims. Next day the Russians staged a repeat performance in Berlin. Even in defeat Keitel could not resist playing the role allocated to him. He attempted to meet the Russians' expectations of a German general by wearing a monocle and, with what Speer called 'a sad lack of dignity and sense of decorum', he drank champagne with the victors after the signing.

But the German general staff did not pass from the historical stage with this inept performance. At the Nuremberg Trial in 1946 the Tribunal which condemned Keitel and Jodl to death for specific crimes, also ruled that the general staff could not be convicted as a criminal organisation. Its planning and operations technique was found to be 'much the same as that of other countries', and it was acquitted.

Keitel signs the surrender documents for the German Army at the Russian HQ in Berlin

Bibliography

Nemesis of Power by J W Wheeler Bennett (McMillan, London)

Der deutsche Generalstabsoffizier Hansgeorg Model (Bernard & Graefe Verlag, Frankfurt aM)

Die Silbernen Spiegel Hermann Teske (Kurt Vowinckel, Heidelberg)

Generaloberst Franz Halder Kriegstagebuch (3 vols.) edited by Hans-Adolf Jacobsen (W Kohlhammer Verlag, Stuttgart)

Kriegstagebuch des OKW (4 vols) edited by Hans-Adolf Jacobsen (Bernard & Graefe Verlag, Frankfurt aM)

Das Heer, 1933-1945 Burckhardt Mueller Hillebrand (E S Mittler & Sohn, Darmstadt)

The Art of Modern War Hermann Foertsch (Oskar Piest, New York)

Inside Hitler's Headquarters Walter Warlimont (Weidenfeld and Nicolson, London)

Lost Victories Erich von Manstein (Methuen, London)

Panzer Leader Heinz Guderian (Michael Joseph, London)

The Rommel Papers edited by B H Liddell Hart (Collins, London)

The Conspiracy against Hitler in the Twilight War Harold C Deutsch (University of Minnesota Press, Minneapolis)

The Sword and Swastika Telford Taylor (Simon and Schuster, New York)

The March of Conquest Telford Taylor (Simon and Schuster, New York)

Politics of the Prussian Army Gordon A Craig (Oxford University Press)